THE FLOWERING SPIRIT

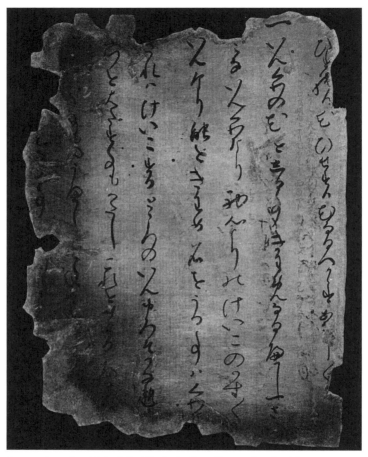

A page from the original *Fūshikaden* in Zeami's own handwriting.

    Understanding the Law of Cause and Effect in relation to the Flower is of the utmost significance. Everything—all things—contains the Law of Cause and Effect. All the many things you have learned about the art of Nō since you were a beginner are the cause. Mastering Nō and gaining a name for yourself is the effect. *Chapter 7, pages 135–6*

THE FLOWERING SPIRIT

CLASSIC TEACHINGS ON THE ART OF NŌ

Zeami

TRANSLATED BY
William Scott Wilson

KODANSHA INTERNATIONAL
Tokyo • New York • London

Note: All Japanese names in this book are written in the Japanese order—that is, with the family name first, followed by the given name.

All translations in this book are by William Scott Wilson unless otherwise noted.

Photo credits: National Noh Theatre.
Jacket photo: Nō mask (*ko-omote*: *bangai*).
Page 152: *Atsumori* performance.

Distributed in the United States by Kodansha America, Inc., and in the United Kingdom and continental Europe by Kodansha Europe Ltd.

Published by Kodansha International Ltd., 17-14 Otowa 1-chome, Bunkyo-ku, Tokyo 112-8652, and Kodansha America, Inc.

English translation copyright © 2006 by William Scott Wilson.
All rights reserved. Printed in Japan.
ISBN-13: 978–4–7700–2499–2
ISBN-10: 4–7700–2499–1

First edition, 2006
15 14 13 12 11 10 09 08 07 06   10 9 8 7 6 5 4 3 2 1

Library of Congress Catalogue-in-Publication Data available.

www.kodansha-intl.com

This translation is dedicated to
the memory of Dana Todd Richardson.

CONTENTS

FOREWORD 9
INTRODUCTION 13
NOTES 56

FŪSHIKADEN, by Zeami 59

Prologue 61

Chapter 1: Concerning Practice and Age 63

    Age Seven 63

    From the Age of Twelve or Thirteen 64

    From the Age of Seventeen or Eighteen 65

    The Age of Twenty-four or Twenty-five 66

    The Age of Thirty-four or Thirty-five 67

    The Age of Forty-four or Forty-five 68

    Beyond the Age of Fifty 69

Chapter 2: Role-playing 71
    Women 72
    Old Men 73
    The Unmasked Face 74
    Madmen 75
    Buddhist Priests 77
    Ashuras 78
    Gods 79
    Demons 79
    Chinese People 80

Chapter 3: Questions and Answers 82

Chapter 4: Matters Concerning the Gods 98

Chapter 5: Praising the Deepest Principles 104

Chapter 6: Cultivating the Flower 112

Chapter 7: Additional Oral Traditions 124

NOTES 140

GLOSSARY 146

ATSUMORI, by Zeami 151

INTRODUCTION 153

NOTES 178

BIBLIOGRAPHY 181

FOREWORD

I saw my first Nō play about thirty-five years ago on the grounds of the Atsuta Shrine in Nagoya, Japan. The memory of that experience, even today, is still vivid: the almost unbelievably slow movements of the demon-masked *shite*, or main actor; the beating of various small drums in unfamiliar rhythms that seemed to evoke dim memories or dreams; the flute emitting sounds more like squeaks than melodies; and the intermittent birdlike cries of the musicians. Plays or operas I had seen growing up in America had always taken me to a different time and place, but they were times and places in this world. The Nō play was very different in that regard.

One other thing that impressed me that day was that almost everyone in the audience of perhaps sixty had copies of the libretto, and was reading along with the performance. This was also quite different from my experience of drama in my own country. What I didn't know at the time was that the language of the play was some six hundred years old, and even if one was conversant with that ancient form, the droning delivery of the actors and the *shite*'s mask obscured the words even further.

Years later, I had the good fortune to take a graduate course in Nō as literature at the University of Washington under the tutelage of Dr. Richard N. McKinnon. Dr. McKinnon had professional connections with a troupe in Japan, and during our class he would periodically stop our reading of the plays and chant the section himself to give us a better understanding of the atmosphere of the material. It was a late-afternoon class and, as dim orange sunlight filtered through the high second-floor windows, I can remember the hair standing up on the backs of our necks. As he chanted, Dr. McKinnon seemed to be almost possessed by someone or something else, but then he would suddenly stop and, with a kind smile, ask us to continue with the reading.

The fundamental handbook translated here, the *Fūshikaden*, has been a sort of bible for Nō actors ever since Zeami Motokiyo perfected the genre and wrote out the notes for it, between 1400 and 1418. It was at first a secret document, so to possess a copy was considered great good fortune—not only by professional actors, but also by the upper echelons of the warrior class. High-ranking samurai practiced the chants, dances, and music of Nō with great enthusiasm, linking this in part to their attainment of high culture, in part to their study of Zen Buddhism, and sometimes even to the art of swordsmanship. The *Fūshikaden* is, even today, read widely enough to require frequent publications and translations into modern Japanese, and offers proof in one slender volume to the oft-quoted statement that "The study of the Nō play is really the study of Japanese culture generally."*

In this regard, a word should be said about the text. It is well known that Zeami's style and vocabulary can be somewhat vague, and translators—rendering the *Fūshikaden* into both English and modern Japanese—are not in agreement as to the meanings of certain terms. To make matters more complicated, Zeami seems to have had a rather fluid sense of definition, so that a word might mean one thing in one section of the book, and something slightly different in another. I have dealt with this problem in part by leaving a few words in the original Japanese and adding a glossary, so that the reader will have a sense of the breadth of a single word; in other cases, I have simply used a more appropriate English term. I have tried to stay as close as possible to the original to convey the range of expression and individual quirks in Zeami's writing. As in all texts of this age, a number of slightly differing versions exist. While relying heavily on the notes and annotations of Nose Asaji's *Zeami jūroku bushū hyōshaku*, I have based the translation on the *Fūshikaden* edited by Nogami Toyoichirō and Nishio Minoru, and published by Iwanami Shoten. The *Atsumori* translation is from the libretto of the twenty-fourth generation Kanze Sakon.

A number of people have given me their assistance in the preparation of this book, and I owe a debt of gratitude to them all: to Kuramochi Tetsuo, senior editor at Kodansha

International, for kindly recommending and supporting this project; to my editor Ginny Tapley for working with me through the rough spots to the bitter end; to Ichikawa Takashi and Agnes Youngblood for generously supplying me with research books that would have otherwise been extremely difficult to obtain; to Kate Barnes, Robin Gill, Gary Haskins, Dr. Daniel Medvedov, Dr. Justin Newman, and John Siscoe for their suggestions and encouragement; and to my wife, Emily, for reading through the entire manuscript and helping to make it more readable. As always, I offer a deep bow of gratitude to my late professors, Prof. Hiraga Noburu and Dr. Richard N. McKinnon. Any and all mistakes are my own.

William Scott Wilson

---

* Suzuki, *Zen and Japanese Culture*, 419.

INTRODUCTION

In the year 1349, a performance of a form of dramatic entertainment known as *dengaku* was to be given in the dry flood plain beside the Kamo River in Kyoto. It is unknown exactly what this performance entailed, but conjecture has it that it included song, dance, and mime, and possibly juggling or acrobatics. What is clear is that *dengaku* was wildly popular at the time, and performances or the promises thereof seemed to elicit a sort of mass hysteria, from wild dancing in the streets to seriously unruly behavior including arson.

This particular performance was to be an extraordinary spectacle: gold brocade curtains were stretched across the stage, which was adorned with the skins of tigers and other exotic beasts; the music of flutes and drums filled the air; and the atmosphere was one of outlandish gaiety. Huge wooden stands had been built to accommodate crowds that included not only the common people, but the aristocracy and even Shōgun Ashikaga Takauji himself.

The program having been announced, the first play was under way when a boy wearing a monkey mask appeared on the stage and the crowd started to get out of hand. As the spectators rushed forward to get a better view, the stands began to tilt and then suddenly collapsed, killing and wounding a great number of people. In the general panic and mayhem that followed, thieves made off with swords, some people were stabbed and robbed, others were scalded by boiling water that had been meant for tea, and young ladies were carried off by local ruffians. In the midst of all this, the *dengaku* actors, still wearing the masks of demons, chased after the thieves, striking at them with red canes. The cries of anguish, the blood and chaos, were no doubt reminiscent of Buddhist descriptions of the torments of hell.

It is likely that one of the spectators of this catastrophe was a sixteen-year-old boy by the name of Yūzaki Saburō, a young actor of another dramatic form called *sarugaku* that was performed during this same period. He had no doubt come to observe the day's event, because *sarugaku* was also composed of song, dance, and mime, and its actors were on good and even cordial terms with the actors of *dengaku*, who were otherwise their rivals. Until the middle of the following century, both theaters were popular, but eventually *dengaku* simply faded away. *Sarugaku*, on the other hand, went on to become the classic theater of Japan and, now called Nō, is still performed today almost exactly as it was six hundred years ago.

As the young Saburō, later known as Kan'ami, retraced his steps to his lodging that day, he must have thought about the courses these two theatrical forms were taking and would have been deeply inspired to move *sarugaku* into a different realm. Creative and poetic, he began to write plays of beauty and depth, experimenting with different forms of music and song. After he died at the age of fifty, his son Zeami took *sarugaku* to even greater subtlety and artistry, so that by the end of the fourteenth century it had become extraordinarily refined and poetic, imbued with Zen Buddhist simplicity and elegance, and at times inspiring the spectators with feelings of religious awe.

As he approached middle age, Zeami wrote down his late father's instructions and thoughts, adding his own astute observations and insights. Although the subject was ostensibly the art of Nō, these writings are informed by the two men's thoughts on what it means to be alive and how to conduct oneself according to the "Way." In this are reflected the primordial religious sentiments of the Japanese, the poetic standards of the aristocracy, Zen Buddhist philosophy, and the warrior class ideals from one of the most creative periods in Japanese history. Zeami entitled this book *Fūshikaden*, literally "Transmission of Style and the Flower," although a broader translation of this title might be "Teachings on Grace and Its Presence." Only one hundred pages in the original, it is still read in Japan today by actors, martial artists, and tea masters in particular, and by the public in general.

What Is Nō?

Nō is a dramatic form comprised essentially of mime or role-playing, poetic chanting, and music. These three are set upon a stage that is bare except for four pillars and a painting of a large pine tree in the background. For some plays a simple prop may be set upon the stage, but it will be reduced to its simplest elements, and understated to the point of mere suggestion. This understatement or suggestion is the essence of the drama itself. All unnecessary complications are swept away, and the primary presence before the spectator is no presence at all, but empty space and time. Thus any words, movements, or sounds—no matter how slight—take on extraordinary significance. The hidden truth of things can be expressed only when sensual illusion is shorn away, and the three elements of Nō are to manifest themselves in exactly this way.

Monomane (Role-playing)

> As regards the two Ways of Being and Non-Being, Being is what is visible, and Non-Being is the vessel. That which manifests Being is Non-Being. A crystal, for example, is clear and transparent in essence, and though its essential voidness has nothing to do with either color or patterns, it can give birth to both fire and water. How is it that both

fire and water, which have different natures, can be produced from a colorless, empty essence?

Yūgaku shūdō fūkensho
Zeami[1]

The central action in Nō is mime or role-playing, which in the *Fūshikaden* is expressed as *monomane*, literally "imitating things." It is performed in extremely spare or symbolic movements and does not aim at realistic depiction, but rather at the very essence of the person, demon, or god being portrayed. This is not a matter of thoughtful expression, but of emptying the mind of ego or self and taking on the true intent of the character being represented. In the *Fūshikaden* Zeami states that when *monomane* is taken to its limits and one truly becomes the object, there is no mind that thinks "I'll imitate this."[2] And in the *Kakyō*,[3] another of his treatises, he declares, "In all *monomane*, no matter what kind of character [you are portraying], you must first learn to become the thing itself." Zeami encourages the actor to take on the "true intent" of the character being imitated, for this is the very essence of *monomane*. All superfluities must be expunged, for only by extreme economy of presentation can that essence be manifest. The audience, too, must watch with the same understanding. In his *Shikadō* treatise, Zeami writes:

> You should know the matter of essence and function in Nō. Essence is like the flower, while function is like the fragrance. Again, this is like the moon

and its light. If you are able to understand essence, function will come into being on its own. Thus, in watching Nō, those who know watch with their minds, while those who don't know watch with their eyes. What is seen with the mind is essence; what is seen with the eyes is function.[4]

Language

Like all actions, language in Nō too is given a distillation or economy that brings it to its most potent. It might be either poetry or prose, but often there is no sharp distinction between the two, and sentences or phrases seem to blend or change from the one to the other. The fundamental rhythm is that of all Japanese poetry, with lines broken into series of five and seven syllables. Phrases are often integrated with poems or segments of poems—either Japanese or Chinese—from ages that were already ancient in Zeami's day, evoking layers of meaning and emotion, one overlapping into another until literal meaning gives way to atmosphere.

The ancient Japanese took it for granted that words, or the proper sequence of words, had the power to move men and the gods. Five hundred years before Zeami, Ki no Tsurayuki stated this clearly in his preface to the *Kokinshū*, one of the most famous of the early anthologies of *waka*, or Japanese poetry:

> It is *waka* that ... without the slightest effort, moves Heaven and Earth, stirs the unseen gods and spirits to feelings of pity, brings accord to husband and wife, and calms the mind of the fierce warrior.[5]

Neither was this belief new with Tsurayuki. The even more ancient prayers called *norito*, which are still chanted today in shrines throughout Japan, have nothing to do with Shintō doctrine but depend on the *kotodama*, or the spiritual power of the words themselves, to effect very practical consequences such as inducing rain, good crops, or the success of an endeavor. Such a mystical power of words was and is believed to bring mental and perhaps even physical purification, and the recitation of such words in rhythmic, double-lined arrangements lacking grammatical and semantic clarity is similar to Nō. Thus poet and priest, recitation and ritual, had unclear boundaries in ancient Japan, and to some extent this is still the case today. It was certainly true in the fourteenth and fifteenth centuries when Zeami was creating his plays and writing the *Fūshikaden*.

The beauty and magic of Zeami's language were well understood and appreciated in his time by all levels of society, from the aristocracy in Kyoto to the common people in the provinces. Its highly literary and poetic quality, combined with an austere Zen Buddhist elegance and almost shamanic associations, could only have had a therapeutic effect on the nation and individual spectators. Words composed and vocalized correctly could bring the sympathy of the gods, calm angry demons, and make right the hearts of all sentient beings. With Zeami's language, *sarugaku*—now Nō—had become transformative, both for this world and the other.

Music

The *Fūshikaden* is fundamentally a manual for actors, and for the most part Zeami focused far less on music. As the third element in Nō, however, some mention should be made of its instruments and style.

Like the role-playing and language, the music in Nō is used with great economy and austerity. Instruments include the *nōkan*—a transverse flute with seven holes, about one foot three inches long; the *kotsuzumi*—a small drum struck with the right hand, carried on the right shoulder supported by the left hand, which controls the pitch by tightening or loosening the tension of the skin; and the *ōkawa* or *ōtsuzumi*—a larger drum held over the left hip and struck with the right hand. In addition, a *taiko*—a large drum supported by a stand and struck with two thick drumsticks—is sometimes used. To these are periodically added the birdlike cries of the drummers. It is minimalist music, encouraging—as do all other aspects of the performance—the imagination of the audience.

During Kan'ami's youth, *sarugaku* rhythms were adapted

mostly from *kouta* or *imayō*, the folk tunes of the day. During the mid-fourteenth century, however, Kan'ami broke with tradition and began to study the *kusemai*, a popular song and dance performed by female entertainers and thought by the more conservative members of the aristocracy to bode the downfall of culture in general. It was Kan'ami's genius to blend the more exotic rhythms of the *kusemai* with those of the softer and more melodic folksongs to produce an almost hypnotic music which, performed with a slower tempo in later years, became the elegant style that is Nō music today.

With this emphasis on rhythm rather than melody, the pauses or empty spaces in the music of Nō have the same emotional import as the sounds they fall between. In the *Yūgaku shūdōfūken*, Zeami quotes the famous phrase of the Buddhist *Prajnaparamita,* or Heart Sutra: "Form is Emptiness, Emptiness is Form" (*shikisokusekū, kūsokuzeshiki,* 色則是空、空則是色). This formula perfectly defines music that emerges from and retreats to emptiness. In Nō, eternal truths are expressed by hints from the deceptive and transitory surfaces of reality, and reality is likewise expressed through eternal truths.

Finally, the framework of the music of Nō is that of *jo*, *ha*, and *kyū*, a principle originally found in Indian music and likely imported to Japan from China from the fifth to the seventh centuries. This concept is used in Nō for everything from the structure of the music itself to the order of plays in a program, and can perhaps be best explained by definitions centering on the kanji characters: *jo* (序), a beginning or introduction, necessarily slow, simple and straightforward, and leading to further stages; *ha* (破), a breakdown of the previous action into more development and complexity; and *kyū* (急), a quickening of the rhythm leading to the climax. In the *Fūshikaden,* Zeami states that, "All things have a *jo*, a *ha*, and a *kyū*, and *sarugaku* is no exception."[6] In his *Shūgyoku tokka,* he elaborated:

> When you think this over well in a tranquil state of mind, you will see that all phenomena in their innumerable forms—good or bad, great and small, sentient and insentient—are, each and every one, endowed with *jo, ha,* and *kyū*. From the twittering of the birds to the cries of the insects, each sings with that principle with which it is provided, and that is *jo, ha,* and *kyū* . . . This [rhythm] is also in the voice of the wind and the sound of water . . .[7]

Jo, ha, and *kyū* is the rhythm governing the music, the performance, and the actors themselves.

The Actors

To the left of the Nō stage is the bridge, or *hashigakari*, along which the actor slowly travels from the "mirror room"[8] to the highly polished floor of the stage. It is the bridge from one world to another, not only for the actor who crosses it, but for the spectators who are themselves led to the place of spirits and anguished ghosts. The actors of Nō, in that sense, are our guides.

There are fundamentally four types of characters that appear in Nō, and the actors who portray each will not likely perform outside that type throughout their lives. They are as follows:

The *waki*. Literally "the one aside," he is often described as the deuteragonist of the play. He is the first to appear, often dressed as a traveler or a simple Buddhist priest, and introduces the general direction of the play. He is, for the most part, an observer of the main character, becoming more involved in the "action" only towards the climax, when he and the main actor pass the chant back and forth with the *waki* in the lead. The *waki* generally does not dance, does not wear a mask, and may be accompanied by an attendant, known as a *tsure* or *wakizure*.

The *shite*, or main character, is the central figure of the play. It is he[9] who the *waki* has come to inquire about due to some previous karmic connection. He appears in a common, everyday form in the first half of the play, and as his "true self" in the second; in the first half he is termed the *maejiite*, and in the second, the *nochijite*. It is the *shite* who dances and chants the most poetic lines, and who often wears a mask. Like the *waki*, he may also be accompanied by as many as seven or eight *tsure*, who may also wear masks. In the second half of the play, the *shite* often wears sumptuous robes which contrast markedly with the simplicity of the stage and its props, concentrating the focus onto the actions and speech of his character. It is the *shite* to whom Zeami refers when he speaks of the "actor," or the "main" or "leading" actor.

The attendants, or *tsure*, may accompany the *waki* and/or the *shite*. They are for the most part unimportant to the storyline and perform the function of a chorus.

The *kyōgen*, literally "crazy words," does not take part in the play proper, but performs a sort of comic role during the interlude between the first and second parts of the play. At the most superficial level, the *kyōgen* simply fills in the interval while the *shite* changes costumes and masks. However, he also relieves some of the tension that has built up during the first half, and fills in the details for those less sophisticated spectators who are not acquainted with the storyline. As the *kyōgen*'s interlude is not considered part of the play proper, his monologue (with some comments from the *waki*) is traditionally included in the libretto in smaller script, if at all.

Masks

The mask worn by the *shite* is the visual fulcrum of the play, and is handled reverently in both its use and its storage. Like Japanese swords, Nō masks are said to have spirits of their own, and thus require utmost respect. Although carved from wood such as Japanese cypress, paulownia, or camphor, and so frozen in expression, they seem to emit subtle emotive changes with slight movements up or down or to the side, especially during *takigi* Nō, which is performed outdoors at night illuminated only by the light of bonfires. The fixed expression of the mask requires that it provide the quintessence of the emotional atmosphere of the play. *Shite* and mask must become one.

Masks had been used in entertainment brought to Japan as early as the seventh century, and these are believed to have originated in places as diverse as Tibet, Central Asia, China, India, and Southeast Asia.[10] They are generally much larger than the Nō masks used by both Zeami and actors nowadays, however, and lack the extraordinary subtlety of expression achieved by these.

In the Nō repertoire today, there are over one hundred different types of masks, ranging from laughing old men to emaciated women, to military commanders and demons, and to fearsome old men and beautiful youths. Regardless of what mask he is wearing, though, the *shite* follows Zeami's injunction to become the character he is miming. Before leaving the mirror room for the *hashigakari*, he sits at length in front of a mirror, absorbing the very essence of the mask, drawing out its life for the few short hours of the play.

The Plays

Nō can be roughly classified into two types: *genzai nō*, or "reality Nō"; and *mugen nō*, or what is commonly called "dream Nō." Some plays, however, seem to straddle these two types and are more difficult to categorize.

Genzai nō deals with the present world of human beings and their affairs, while the story unfolds in conformity with real time. This kind of Nō is sometimes termed *ōdōbanriyū* (横道萬里雄), or "Heroes Going a Thousand Leagues Down the Wrong Path," which nicely summarizes the storyline of a number of these plays. Love, attachment to the past, demented psychological states, and possession are typical of these plays, yet the atmosphere is still of this world.

Mugen nō, on the other hand, deals entirely with the world of illusion, the world of spirits and ghosts where the barriers between dream and reality, life and death, are indistinct. This style of Nō was perfected by Zeami, who was strongly influenced by Buddhism. He probably took the term *mugen* (夢幻), "dreams and illusions," from the verse in the last chapter of the *Vajracchedika*, or Diamond Sutra, which states:

> All phenomena are
>   like a dream (夢), an apparition (幻), a bubble,
>   or a shadow;
> They are like dew, or again, like lightning.
> Hence, you should view them like this.

This is Buddhism in a nutshell. The Diamond Sutra has traditionally been considered the vehicle for seeing into one's own nature, and it may have been Zeami's desire that *mugen nō* follow this ideal.

In *mugen nō*, the *waki* is a traveler, often a vagrant monk whose station is somewhere between priest, shaman, and beggar. By the very fact that he journeys alone through the country, he is on equal footing with wandering spirits, street preachers, prostitutes, and those who fall somewhere in between. This monk is usually visiting a place with which he has some karmic connection, and there he encounters the *shite* in the role of a god, or the soul of a dead person, who has taken on a human form. The latter will tell the monk a story historically connected with the place, hint that he may be someone other than who he appears to be, and then fade away. An interlude follows, in which the *kyōgen* gives a prosaic summary of the story that in the play is presented mostly in poetic terms. In the second half of the play, the *shite* reappears, now in his authentic form, and chants with gestures as he recalls the events of his past, exposing his own anguish and attachments. As the *shite* dances to express his deep emotions, the monk prays and then confronts the ghost, moving him to transcend the psychological state barring him from salvation. The play ends with a cathartic dance by the *shite*, releasing him from his anger and grief.

In these plays it is not at all clear where reality ends and dream begins. Was the entire drama conjured up by the monk in meditation, or had parts of the play simply been his own reverie?

The tension of *mugen nō* is felt intensely by the audience, and is created not by the interplay between *waki* and *shite*, but by the *shite*'s own inner torment, by the conflict between his anger and attachment to past events, and the possibility of salvation through release of that attachment. It is a tension created by the contradiction of a Buddhist understanding of the transience of things and the inability to let go of the past. The *shite* moves back and forth between the worlds on either side of his own death until the *waki*—a man who understands both worlds—is able to bring him to a catharsis and to his release and purification.

The spectators, too, feel this effect and the anguish and spiritual transition of the *shite* as their own. The play is over like "a dream, an apparition, a bubble, or a shadow."

Within the two general classifications of *genzai* and *mugen nō*, there are five categories of plays. These include god plays, in which the *shite* portrays a god or goddess; warrior plays, in which the *shite* plays a famous figure from the *Heike monogatari* ("The Tale of the Heike") or other early warrior epics; "wig" plays, in which the *shite* usually plays a young or beautiful woman; miscellaneous plays, which usually involve stories of ordinary men and women moved to madness or grief; and demon plays, in which the *shite* portrays some supernatural being. These categories are ordinarily arranged in the principle of *jo, ha,* and *kyū* for extended performances, with the god plays serving as the *jo*, the three middle categories the *ha*, and the demon plays the *kyū*.

In a class all by themselves are the *Okina*, or "Old Man" plays, which are peformed only on special occasions such as the New Year. These are called the *Shiki sanbon*—the "Three Ceremonial Pieces"—and portray the three gods Okina, Senzai, and Sanbaso. Zeami did not write these plays—they seem to date from the twelfth century—but he held them in special reverence. In some sections as vague and unintelligible as *norito* prayers, they are performed with a religious sensibility, almost always in joyful thanks to the gods being portrayed. The actors playing these gods will first go through a ritual purification, take a cup of sacred saké at an altar in the mirror room before departing for the *hashigakari*, and pray to be filled with the spirit of the god inhabiting its mask.

The repertoire of Nō confirms Zeami's assertion in the *Fūshikaden* that the dramas serve as prayers for the peace and prosperity of the whole country, and that they have the power to pacify the minds of heretics and demons. Whether through the Buddhist salvation of troubled ghosts or the joyful celebration of Shintō gods, the plays have always provided audiences with artistic, spiritual, and historical cultural experiences of astonishing depth.

Background

Origins

In the *Fūshikaden*, Zeami gives us two versions of the origin of Nō: one Shintō, one Buddhist. This is appropriate as both religions influenced the underlying meaning of the plays and their style. Despite centuries of research, however, scholars are still not agreed on exactly how Nō developed into its classical form. Zeami himself states that "time has passed, and with the interposition of the ages it no longer lies within our abilities to learn how it first appeared."[11]

Objects of physical culture had likely been coming to Japan from the continent since the earliest times: pottery, textiles, and other material goods were brought down through the Korean peninsula and across the Straits of Tsushima for trade. Then, in the fifth and sixth centuries, Japan was culturally enriched by the Chinese written language with its accompanying thousand years of literature, and Buddhism with its equally long traditions, holy books, and sculptures. The Chinese language and Buddhism certainly helped to create a high level of sophistication at the imperial court, although it did not immediately filter down to the lower levels of society.

Those lower tiers of Japanese society were reached in the seventh and eighth centuries, possibly as early as 612, with the importation of the courtly ritual dances of *gigaku* and *bugaku*. At the same time, various forms of popular entertainment called *sangaku* (散楽, *san-yueh* in Chinese) were introduced and began their rise to immense popularity. *Sangaku*, which included mime, song, dance, and acrobatics, was first performed as a sort of comic relief after the stately religious Shintō dances called *kagura*, and was so well received by the court that it established a special school—the Sangakkō—for its study by the early eighth century. Its popularity quickly spread to all levels of society, and the class-conscious court then abolished the school in 782. Cut off from their support, the performers went on to secure the patronage of Buddhist temples and Shintō shrines, where they were obliged to perform during special observances and festivals. At other times the actors would go "on the road," supplementing their income with performances in villages and towns outside of the capital. Although allied to sacred institutions and influenced by both Buddhism and Shintō, *sangaku* would for a long while retain a relatively secular aura. Eventually it became known as *sarugaku*, an appellation arrived at by removing the left-hand radical (ネ) from the character meaning "divine" (神) in *kagura* (神楽), to leave the right-hand radical (申), which means "to speak" and is pronounced *saru*. By the second half of the eleventh century, entertainment included under the general title of *sarugaku* included tightrope-walking, puppetry, juggling balls and knives, and *dengaku*.

Dengaku (田楽), literally "field music," began as songs and dances performed by villagers during rice planting, both to please the gods to ensure good harvests, and to relieve the tedium of the work. Catching the attention of the aristocracy, these songs and dances were eventually performed in an appropriately refined manner at the court, and at temples and shrines. In this way, *dengaku* was from the beginning associated with fertility, life force, and sexuality, and may have eventually been linked with the spirit-possession of Shintō priestesses. From the eleventh century, *dengaku* and *sarugaku* developed along parallel paths, their actors mutually influencing each other, until both had evolved into genres involving mime, dance, and song. Both eventually used the word *nō* (能) in the sense of "performance," hence the terms *sarugaku nō* and *dengaku nō*.

By the fourteenth century, other more bizarre entertainments such as the *kusemai* and *shirabyōshi*—songs and dances by female performers—had become popular as well. This was a time of public performances by female prostitutes, entertainers called *yūjo*, traveling troupes of actors, and proselytizing nuns and priests who both preached and entertained, and whose status was often ambivalent at best. Anyone on the road (*michi no mono*) who was not tied to any community, either rural or urban, was thought to have some connection with the supernatural, such as foxes or raccoon dogs (*tanuki*), which were known to bewitch the unwary, or other strange spirits that might be traveling with them. In the fifth chapter of the *Taiheiki*, a fourteenth-century chronicle, there is an interesting entry concerning some *dengaku* actors who had been invited into a castle to provide entertainment.

> A certain female attendant heard their voices and, overcome with interest, peeked in at them through a tear in the paper doors. What she saw of the Shinza and Honza *dengaku* actors was that none of them had a human shape, but all had strange apparitional forms of black-eared kites, or *yamabushi*.[12] Astonished, this female attendant had a man run to inform Adachi Tokiaki. Hearing this, Tokiaki grabbed a long sword, but when the strange beings heard his rough footsteps coming through the central gate, they disappeared without a trace . . . Taking up a lamp, Tokiaki looked over the place where the festivities had been held, and it did appear as though it had truly been a gathering place for *tengu*.[13] On the trampled and dirtied floor were a great number of bird and animal tracks.[14]

By the time of the disastrous *dengaku* performance in Kyoto in 1349 when the seating collapsed, or even possibly before then, serious *sarugaku* actors—Kan'ami foremost among them—must have felt a strong desire to distance themselves from the bizarre and flashy, albeit more popular, *dengaku* of the day.

Although the source material of the two genres was probably quite similar by this time, from this point on *sarugaku* would place more emphasis on artistic beauty and spiritual significance than on the spectacular and arousing. *Dengaku* and *sarugaku* actors would continue to respect and admire each other until *dengaku*'s eventual demise in the late fifteenth century. However, *sarugaku* now moved towards something more reserved and rarified, a drama less influenced by the earthy, unrestrained spiritualism of Shintō than by the unearthly, transcendent spirit of Buddhism—Zen Buddhism in particular.

Buddhism

Buddhism was introduced to Japan via Korea around the middle of the sixth century, and already had a history of at least a thousand years in Asia. The Buddha's message was that life is unsatisfactory, and that we suffer because of our ignorance, greed, and hate. His fundamental solution encompassed a radical rejection of attachment—from physical objects to notions of self and what the universe is—and universal compassion. Foremost among the methods he advocated for reaching a deep understanding of why we should reject attachment and embrace compassion was sitting quietly in meditation. The state reached in obtaining this understanding has been called *satori* (悟), the kanji character of which is composed of the radicals for "mind" and "I." It is generally said to mean understanding one's deepest nature, which is also known as enlightenment.

The Buddhism that first reached Japan was far more complicated than this simple synopsis. Six sects arrived within decades of each other, representing sophisticated systems of argument concerning the various concepts of enlightenment, descriptions of various mental and psychological states, and the innumerable rules for becoming a monk or nun, and so forth, that had developed over the thousand years since the Buddha's death. Just as importantly, they were imported into Japan as part of the cosmopolitan Chinese package—including a written language, literature, governmental systems, architecture, and more—that the Japanese court was taking on wholesale. The virtue of the Buddhism that arrived at this time thus lay largely in the power and prestige of the Chinese culture that it represented. Certainly most of the aristocracy at the time had no deep understanding of it, and possibly many of the priests—men selected from the sons of the aristocracy—had little idea of what they were getting into. The temples, ceremonies, elaborate sutra readings, and fine robes, however, attracted attention, and the basic concept of the new religion slowly began to filter down.

In the ninth century, two new kinds of Buddhism were brought back to Japan by Japanese monks who had studied in China. The Tendai sect taught by Dengyō Daishi (also known as Saichō, 767–822) attempted to synthesize all previous Buddhist teachings, categorizing them according to their level of spiritual truth, and stressed the ideas of totality and the interpenetration of those truths. It emphasized mandalas, mudras, and esoteric ceremonies.

The Shingon school was taught by Kōbō Daishi (Kūkai, 774–835), and placed special emphasis on the mysteries of the body, speech, and mind. The rituals and ceremonies of Shingon were for the most part secret, but some were occasionally performed in public, much to the fascination and enjoyment of the spectators. Most importantly, especially in terms of the origins of Nō, Shingon adherents believed that the true, or deepest, meanings of Buddhism could not be taught by words, but only through artistic representation, which also included mandalas, mudras, and mantras.

The practice of using art—visual, vocal, and physical—to approach or express truth were readily accepted by the Japanese, who already had the tradition of the ancient *norito* prayers that through the spiritual power of words and their arrangements could move the gods. Both Shintō and Buddhism can accommodate the concept that this world and the other are not so distinctly defined as in religions such as Christianity, Judaism, or Islam, and that both worlds constantly interact and interpenetrate. Body, speech, and mind, so important to Zeami and his art, were not considered as temporal, earthly, or limited as we in the West might think of them today. According to the Tendai and Shingon sects, these "three mysteries" can bring us into contact with other realms and other beings, be they Buddhas or spirits. The power of body, speech, and mind to transcend the boundary between this world and the other is the subtle but persistent undercurrent of Zeami's writings on Nō, and of the dramas themselves.

Zen Buddhism

Zen was first introduced to the Japanese Buddhist world through Eisai (1141–1215), who mixed elements of Tendai and Shingon practices with his Zen, due either to pressure from other established schools of Buddhism, or perhaps to his own particular style. In the early thirteenth century, however, Zen was given a new impetus by Dōgen (1200–53), who became the most important and influential Zen master in Japan.

Zen, in general, sweeps away all before it but the concentrated mind. The mind may be concentrated on a koan,[15] or on itself. Dōgen stressed the latter style, called *shikantaza*, which emphasizes that the mind should be concentrated and alert, but free from any images or thoughts. In this sense, it is important to recall that the kanji character for Zen is written 禅, which breaks down to "manifesting" (示) the "simple" (単). No mantras, no mudras, no mandalas—and in classic Chinese Zen not even any reliance on sutras. The Zen monk brings himself to and manifests the very essence of "being/not-being" (*yu/mu*, 有/無). In this way, the Zen saying "Sweep your garden, no matter how small" is generally considered to refer to the mind, but it may be applied to many of the Zen-influenced arts as well. The simplicity and near-emptiness of the tearoom, the all-but-empty stage of the Nō drama, the vast empty spaces in *sumi-e* ink paintings, and the clarity and spareness of Zen temple gardens are but a few well-known examples. With Dōgen's Zen, religion, art, and lifestyle all reflected the ideal of "manifesting the simple," and thereby the very essence of life. Zeami, in particular, was affected by these ideals.

But it was not just the simplicity and elegance of Zen that attracted Zeami; he was well acquainted with its deepest concepts as well. Certainly his writings on Nō and his dramas themselves are replete with Zen phrases, words, and allusions. In the *Fūshikaden*, for example, Zeami consistently refers to the study of Nō as a Way (*michi*, 道), rather than simply an art or a way of making a living.[16] He repeatedly refers to the practice of Nō as a religious discipline, the realization of which is the performance. But Zeami makes no distinction between practice and performance, reflecting Dōgen's dictum that "To think that practice and realization are not one is the view of heretics. In Buddhism, practice and realization are the same."[17] When Zeami states that "Life has an end, but Nō has no end," he is again echoing Dōgen: "Because practice itself is realization, there is no end to realization; because realization itself is practice, there is no beginning to practice."[18]

Zeami also often employed the Zen concept of "no-mind"

(*mushin*, 無心), declaring it to be the finest level of performance and practice of *monomane*. This again points to one of Dōgen's most famous teachings:

> To study Buddhism is to study the self. To study the self is to forget the self. To forget the self is to be actualized by all phenomena. When actualized by all phenomena, your own body and mind, as well as the bodies and minds of others, will be molted away.[19]

Zeami was remarkably erudite, not only in his knowledge of Japanese poetic literature, but also in the depth of Zen literature. In his dramas, it is interesting that he often had old crones lecturing Zen to laymen or even to priests of other sects, as in *Sotoba Komachi* and *Yamanba*. In the latter play, the old mountain crone repeats a Zen phrase on non-duality, "Good and evil are not two" (*zen'aku funi*, 善悪不二), and later recites through the chorus:

> When you see the similarity of
>   the heretical and the correct,
>   it is just like "Form is Emptiness."
> If there is a Buddhist Law,
>   there is a Law for this world;
> If there are worldly passions, then
>   enlightenment exists.

Zeami's fourteenth-century Kyoto audience would not have missed this reference to non-duality, and might think that Zeami's Nō, as Zen, "is like a hammer striking the Void—before and after, its mysterious sounds going everywhere."[20]

Much as the aristocracy had taken to the Tendai and Shingon sects, attracted in part by their colorful ceremonies and rites and perhaps equally by their esoteric qualities, the warrior class was now drawn to this new sect of Zen. In sweeping away everything unessential, Zen goes straight to the question of life and death, understandably important to the warrior. Zen relies far more on meditation and direct intuition than on discourse and reasoning, and so would be much more suited to making quick battlefield decisions. The Hōjō regents, warrior rulers of Japan throughout the thirteenth and much of the fourteenth centuries, were enthusiastic students of Zen; it was the regent Tokimune's solving of the famous koan "Jōshū's Dog" that gave him the tranquility of mind to successfully expel the Mongol invasions of 1274 and 1281. Zen became the de facto religion of the warrior class in the thirteenth century, and by the fourteenth it was an integral part of its culture.

Zeami

It was when Zen became secularized through its association with the arts—Nō, tea, and swordsmanship, for example—

that it truly became Zen, rather than just another self-conscious religion with all the trappings, bald-pated priests, scriptures, incense, and rituals. When asked the meaning of Zen, its first patriarch Bodhidharma replied, "Nothing holy, just a vast blue sky"—a reference to "no-mind." It was the father and son team of Kan'ami and Zeami who first applied this to what is now considered the classical theater of Japan.

Kan'ami Kiyotsugu was born in Iga no Kuni (now Mie Prefecture) in 1333, the year of the founding of the Ashikaga or Muromachi Shogunate.[21] As the head of the Yūzaki-za *sarugaku* troupe, he both traveled to the communities around the Kyoto area and was contracted to perform at certain temples and shrines in the capital. Actors, however, were considered by the aristocrats to be little better than beggars, and were thought of as *majiwaranu hito* (people with whom one does not mix) by the townspeople where they performed. But Kan'ami seems to have been a rare type: perusal of his plays shows him to have been well versed in the finer points of classical poetry and Zen Buddhism; one of his childhood playmates became an important and scholarly Zen priest, and tradition has it that he was a cousin or nephew of Kusunoki Masashige (1294–1336), the great warrior who fought for the restoration of the emperor Go-Daigo, and who is often held up as an example of the perfect samurai. It is also thought that Kan'ami performed priestly functions at the Kasuga Shrine that went beyond his *sarugaku* performances. Whatever his background, Kan'ami seems to have been an extraordinary actor and a creative writer and director. He revolutionized *sarugaku* by mixing it with the better elements of *dengaku* and the *kusemai* dance, and laid the foundation of Nō.

In 1374, Kan'ami and his eleven-year-old son, Zeami, gave a performance of *sarugaku* in the Kyoto district of Imagumano. Among the spectators was Ashikaga Yoshimitsu, the third Ashikaga shōgun and one of the most distinguished men in the history of Japan. Before his death at the age of fifty, Yoshimitsu (1358–1408) transformed Kyoto into a cultural, military, and religious center; and through his sponsorship of Zen Buddhism and the arts that we now think of as exemplifying Japanese culture, he made the two nearly synonymous. This is all the more remarkable since at the time many of those arts were considered lowbrow.

Yoshimitsu was only eighteen years old when he attended the performance at Imagumano, but what he saw led him immediately to offer sponsorship to Kan'ami's troupe. This had two main implications for Kan'ami, and subsequently for his son: firstly, although they would continue to perform in rural venues, they no longer had to rely upon income from these performances; and secondly, they now began to imbue their plays with an even higher literary content and the Zen vocabulary that was the lingua franca of their sponsor.

For Zeami, this turn of events brought more than just economic and creative freedom. Yoshimitsu had been astonished by Zeami's acting, and was charmed even further upon his personal acquaintance. To the shock of many aristocrats, he began to invite father and son to his residence, and enjoyed having the boy in his company at cultural events, or simply at his leisure. This relationship exposed Zeami to the refined culture at the highest echelon of Kyoto aristocratic society, and gave him an opportunity to study under some of the most gifted men of his age, including the master of linked poetry Nijō Yoshimoto, who quickly perceived the boy's potential. Zeami became conversant with the classical literature of Japan, as well as familiar with the more intimate aspects of daily life in the court. Even the nobles who still regarded actors as nothing more than *michi no mono* likely felt compelled to encourage and favor Zeami, since Yoshimitsu's example would not have been ignored.

In the year 1384, Kan'ami died during a performance in the countryside, and Zeami took on the responsibility of leading the Yūzaki troupe. The son had idolized his father, whose death now impressed upon him the transience of life, and he enrolled at Fuganji Temple under the abbot Ryōdō Shingaku, his father's childhood friend. Zeami likely studied there under Taiyō Bonsei, one of the abbot's leading disciples and a scholar on Dōgen's lifetime work, the *Shōbōgenzō*. Dōgen's emphasis on *shitsu'u busshō* (悉有仏性), or the universality of the Buddha Nature, combined with Taiyō Bonsei's erudition and sense of compassion, must have affected Zeami, whose plays depicting the purification of a ghost's karma proved cathartic for the audience itself. If all things shared the Buddha Nature, could not the plays of *sarugaku* one day become the vehicles of purification as well?

Zeami had received a heavy dose of secularized Zen at Yoshimitsu's residence, and now at the Fuganji he was exposed to the true classics of Zen. Although emphasis would have been laid on the works of Dōgen, he must also have read almost daily from the Heart, Diamond, and Platform Sutras, and worked through many of the classics of Zen literature. Quotes from these later appeared throughout both his plays and his treatises on Nō.

As the head of the Yūzaki troupe, however, Zeami could not be at the Fuganji continuously. From 1385 or so, he was heavily involved in performing, and in writing new plays and rewriting older ones. In the year 1400, he began his first and most famous treatise, the *Fūshikaden*, which took him some eighteen years to complete. Over the years he wrote at least another fifteen treatises,[22] and up to one hundred plays. He also married and fathered at least two sons and one daughter.

In the year 1408, Zeami lost his greatest benefactor with the death of the Shōgun Ashikaga Yoshimitsu. Although Yoshimitsu had found other favorites over the years, he had continued to sponsor Zeami's troupe, and the aura of his authority and prestige insured the troupe's continuance and prosperity. Yoshimitsu's successor, Ashikaga Yoshimochi (1386–1428), had actually assumed the position of shōgun in 1394 while his father focused his attention on the construction of his famous retirement villa at Kitayama and other pursuits. Yoshimochi's tastes ran more toward *dengaku* and its most famous actor of the time, Zoami, and the court followed his lead.

Although the popularity of Zeami's troupe now declined, Zeami himself continued to be active as an actor and writer, and around 1422 he also became a lay monk. In 1428 Yoshimochi died and was succeeded by his brother Yoshinori (1393–1441), and it was at this point that Zeami's fortunes turned for the worse.

The matter of succession has always presented problems everywhere in the world, and it is no different in Japan, where various issues have caused dissent within the imperial family, the shogunate, clans, and in acting troupes, too. This is understandable when the continuance of a line depends on its leader, as it did with Zeami's troupe, by then known as the Kanze[23] troupe. Zeami himself stated this clearly in the *Fūshikaden*:

> [The oral teachings] should not be given to someone without talent, even if he is your child. As the saying goes, "A birthright is not the clan. The clan is the handing down of the art. A man is not necessarily *the* man. It is knowledge that makes him so."[24]

Earlier in his career, there seems to have been some doubt

that Zeami would produce an heir capable of succeeding the first two patriarchs of the troupe, and he spent much time and attention on his nephew On'ami, whom he considered quite talented and who was already a favorite among some of the aristocrats. However, a rift between On'ami and Zeami turned disastrous when Yoshinori officially sponsored On'ami rather than Zeami himself. Two years later, Zeami suffered a further loss when his son Motoyoshi gave up the art to become a Buddhist priest. Zeami's greatest catastrophe, however, came when his other son Motomasa, the head of the Kanze troupe since 1429 and a superb actor, died in 1432. Zeami was devastated, and wrote that the future of his troupe had all but collapsed.

Zeami's one remaining beacon of hope was his son-in-law Zenchiku, a member of the Konparu troupe, whom he now came to see as the future of his line. Zenchiku was an excellent actor and playwright, and it was to him that Zeami entrusted all of his secret writings, the *Fūshikaden* included. These writings had been at the center of a dispute for some time. As early as 1429, Yoshinori had strongly suggested that they be handed over to On'ami, but Zeami refused. As retribution, Zeami and his son Motomasa had been prohibited by shogunal decree from appearing at the palace of the ex-emperor, or even on its grounds.

Finally, for reasons unknown, but likely because of his continued refusal to give up his secret writings, Zeami was banished to the remote Sado Island, a traditional place of exile in the Japan Sea. The year was 1434, and Zeami was seventy-one or seventy-two. Consistent with his Buddhist views that life was but a dream or an illusion, and that all things contain the Buddha Nature, Zeami seemed to take his banishment in stride. His final treatise was a short travelogue of his journey to Sado Island, called the *Kintōsho* (金島書), or "Book of the Golden Isle"; written with sensitivity, elegance and beauty, it embodies the Zen phrase, "Every day is a good day."

This is the last we hear of him. When Yoshinori died in 1441, an amnesty was declared, and it is thought that perhaps Zeami returned to the capital at that time or soon thereafter. All that is known with certainty is that he died in 1443 at the age of eighty or eighty-one.

The Kanze troupe split into two while Zeami and Motomasa were still alive. The Kyō-Kanze, or the official troupe of Kyoto, was headed by On'ami, while the Ochi-Kanze, which took its name from its base in Ochi Village in Yamato Province, was headed by Motomasa until his death. Although the secret texts remained in the possession of the Ochi-Kanze, the troupe ceased to exist after the first half of the sixteenth century. The texts were then copied down by top members of the Kyō-Kanze. Thus, the leaders of the Kanze troupe founded by Kan'ami and Zeami have ever since been the descendants of On'ami.

The Fūshikaden

Discovery

Zeami wrote the *Fūshikaden* between the years 1400 and 1418. It was his intention that it be a secret text summing up the experiences and thoughts concerning *sarugaku*—or Nō, as it came to be known—of his father Kan'ami and himself as the founders of the Kanze school. At the time, the Kanze school was competing with other schools of *sarugaku* and *dengaku*, and Zeami believed that success depended in great part on secrecy. Thus it was intended only for a particular group of actors and playwrights, to secure the continuance of that group.

Zeami and Kan'ami had seen enough of the other schools at that time to understand that their own continued success and survival would not depend solely on technique. Zeami wrote that "The Mind is the Flower, the seed is technique,"[25] and the *Fūshikaden* was meant to lead the actor to that proper Mind—to serve as an approach to the Way, not to just another art.

The *Fūshikaden* did not remain a secret for long, however. It passed into the possession of the Kyō-Kanze group some time around the middle of the sixteenth century. Not fifty years later, Kanze Jūrō, the Nō teacher to Tokugawa Ieyasu—who became the first shōgun of the Edo era—presented him with a number of Zeami's texts. Ieyasu, in turn, loaned his copies to the daimyō and poet Hosokawa Yūsai, and the descendants of these two men would pass copies on to others, including the sword masters they so admired, Yagyū Munenori and possibly even the great Miyamoto Musashi.

Although the *Fūshikaden* was current among the upper echelons of warrior society and their friends, it was not available to the public at large. It was not until 1908, when a collection of Zeami's texts was discovered in a secondhand bookstore, that they were edited and published the following year. Gradually, other texts and versions of those texts began to surface. By 1940, the definitive set of sixteen of Zeami's treatises were collected, annotated, and translated into modern Japanese by the scholar Nose Asaji, and published as the *Zeami jūroku bushū*, or "The Sixteen Treatises of Zeami." Since then, more scholarship has been dedicated to the *Fūshikaden*, and new publications continue to this day. Although Zeami wrote that the book was absolutely not written "for the purpose of other people becoming more erudite,"[26] it has become a classic for people wishing to have a deeper understanding of Nō and all that it represents.

The Title

In the first section of chapter 5, Zeami states: "In the continuation of our style, the Flower is passed down from mind to mind, and so I have named this book *Fūshikaden* (風姿花伝)."[27] This translates as "The Transmission of Style and the Flower," which seems straightforward enough except that with Zeami these terms always seem to be in a state of flux. The word *fūshi* (風姿), for example, is most often translated as "style," but as one reads through the *Fūshikaden*, the word begins to morph slightly to suggest perhaps "a manifested or expressed form," "an atmosphere," or quite often "a presence." If characters in Zeami's plays could move from one world to another, his vocabulary, too, was free from rigid constraints.

The word *hana* (花), or "flower," is another example. The concept of the Flower might be loosely defined as a condition of the performance that creates a unique impression or sensation of charm and beauty for the audience. This may seem abstract, but Zeami himself never clearly defines the term, although it is at the very heart of the *Fūshikaden*. The closest he comes is when he states that "The Flower, that which is interesting, and that which is unique—these three are the same at the heart of the matter."[28] At the beginning of the book, *hana* seems to imply "grace," in both the physical and the spiritual sense; but this changes, too, and one begins to see that, for Zeami, a concept so important would lose its vitality if too strictly defined. Furthermore, over the eighteen years it took for Zeami to write this short book, his ideas regarding these words and the concepts they represented likely changed.

The alternative title of this work is simply *Kadensho* (花伝書), or "The Book of the Transmission of the Flower"—not to be confused with *kadensho* (家伝書), which refers to a family history or tradition. With this title, Zeami alluded to the story of the first transmission of Zen by the Buddha Shakyamuni to his disciple Mahakasyapa, related in Case 6 of the *Mumonkan* (無門関), a book of koans Zeami would have known through his study of Zen.

> Long ago, when the World-Honored One held a meeting on Mt. Grdhrakuta, he twirled a flower before all the monks. At that time, they all remained silent, and only Mahakasyapa broke into a smile. The World-Honored One said, "I have the Treasure Eye of the True Dharma (*shōbōgenzō*, 正法眼蔵), the Mysterious Heart of Nirvana, the True Form of No-Form, and the Subtle Gate of the Law. Without standing on words and letters, and with a special transmission beyond the teachings, these are bequeathed to Mahakasyapa."[29]

This was the original "Flower passed down from Mind to Mind"—*ishin denshin* (以心伝心) in Zen parlance—and with this title Zeami expresses the supreme importance he places on his book.

Composition

The *Fūshikaden* is the first book to both address and attempt to elucidate Nō. It comprises seven chapters on differing subjects, and formulates a thesis covering the whole of Nō within a broad field of reference. The chapters are not uniform: statements on techniques, questions and answers in the Zen style, and histories written in quite a different style reflect Zeami's own evolution over the eighteen years of the book's composition.

CHAPTER 1: PRACTICE AND AGE divides an actor's life into seven periods, from age seven to past fifty, and articulates a basic course of appropriate practice for each period. "Practice" encompasses both the performance on the stage and the mental effort the actor exerts. The actor is admonished from the beginning to "put strength into [his] practice and avoid conceit," and to adhere to this throughout his career.

CHAPTER 2: ROLE-PLAYING divides role-playing or *monomane*—the basis of the Nō performance—into nine categories: women, old men, the unmasked face, madmen, Buddhist priests, Ashuras, gods, demons, and Chinese people. It also emphasizes the grasp of the "main intention," details of impersonation, and even the costume of each role.

CHAPTER 3: QUESTIONS AND ANSWERS contains nine questions and their answers, explaining such things as the effort necessary for making the Flower bloom, the beauty of Nō, the various ranks in the art, dramatic presentation, and the proper way to write plays. It also emphasizes the importance of the True Flower—one not affected by age or anything else—over the Temporary Flower, or the beauty of appearance and voice possessed simply by virtue of youth. This expository writing by means of questions and answers was typical of the "transmission books" (*densho*, 伝書) of this period; such books included the *Tsukuba mondō*, Nijō Yoshimoto's book on linked poetry, and the *Muchū mondō*, Musō Soseki's book on Zen, both of which Zeami had likely seen.

CHAPTER 4: MATTERS CONCERNING THE GODS explains the beginnings of Nō in both Shintō and Buddhist terms. The style of this chapter differs somewhat from the others, and there is some speculation that it was borrowed from the traditional histories of various troupes. It is notable that Zeami accepts both traditions without preference for one over the other, but states in the very first section of the book that "time has passed, and with the interposition of the ages it no longer lies within our abilities to learn how [Nō] first appeared."[30]

CHAPTER 5: PRAISING THE DEEPEST PRINCIPLES emphasizes that the Flower is the very life of Nō. It states that achieving the Flower is common to Ōmi *sarugaku* and *dengaku*, and stresses the necessity of being able to perform in a broad range of styles. It explains that "the love and respect of the people" is one and the same as the "longevity and prosperity of the troupe," and explains how this can be cultivated.

CHAPTER 6: CULTIVATING THE FLOWER is a transmission addressed to the future leaders of the Kanze school. Its central theme is the actual writing of plays and the fundamental problems involved. It also examines what makes a play superior or inferior, and how to perform plays of varying quality.

In this chapter, Zeami deals with the proper mentalities of actors, particularly the *shite*.

CHAPTER 7: ADDITIONAL ORAL TRADITIONS explains how to win in competitions with other troupes. It is generally a discussion of the Flower, its true meaning, how it can be conditioned by cause and effect, good moments and bad moments within a performance, and the importance of secrecy: "If it is hidden, it is the Flower."[31] Finally, Zeami emphasizes that all these secret matters should be transmitted with extreme care and only to the appropriate person.

Reading the Fūshikaden

Nō is one of the arts most representative of Muromachi period Japan, one of the most serendipitously creative eras in world history. It was a period when art, religion, and everyday life in Japan became unified in a cultural sense, when the secularization of Zen Buddhism brought new meaning to the the famous phrase, "The everyday mind, this is the Way" (*byōjōshin koredō*, 平常心是道). The Way of Nō, the Way of Tea, and even the seeds for the Way of Haiku developed during this time, spreading Zen-inspired culture to a great cross section of society. Appreciating Nō required the most education of the three, specifically in classical literature, but Zeami continually stressed that performances should always be appropriate to the audience and venue.

Just as appreciation of the Way of Haiku includes reading the verses in the appropriate spirit,[32] and the Way of Tea encompasses tasting powdered tea from a ceramic bowl, a full appreciation of Nō must include attending a performance or a number of performances having done the appropriate homework.

But in the *Fūshikaden*, Zeami gives us a framework not only for understanding the drama itself, but also for delving into a Way that has permeated the cultural life of Japan for over six hundred years. Just as members of the warrior class found time not only to attend Nō performances, but to practice its chants, dances, and musical instruments, Japanese businessmen, housewives, and students today still do the same.

Zeami developed the Way of Nō through his experiences with *sarugaku*, *dengaku*, itinerant Buddhist monks, warriors, and likely some dodgy travelers on the road; he deepened the Way through his association with Shintō priests, through long, uncomfortable hours of silent, seated meditation, and through his affiliations with some of the most powerful and cultured men and women of his day. The *Fūshikaden* gives us a window through which to perceive this Way; it is a guide to otherwise hidden aspects of Japan, reaching to a past before Zeami and into worlds other than our own.

NOTES

1. Nose, *Zeami jūroku būshū hyōshaku*, vol. 1, 536.
2. See page 128.
3. Nose, *Zeami jūroku būshū hyōshaku*, vol. 1, 295.
4. Ibid., 467. For an interesting parallel, see Yagyū, *Life-Giving Sword*, 121.
5. Kojima & Arai, *Kokin wakashū*, 4.
6. See page 85.
7. Katō & Omote, *Zeami, Zenchiku*, 191.
8. *Kagami no ma*: literally "mirror room," this is the area backstage where the actors prepare themselves mentally and physically for the performance.
9. All acting in Nō—male and female roles—is performed by men.
10. Incredibly, a number of the Asian masks still exist today in Japanese museums.
11. See page 61.
12. *Yamabushi*: literally, "those who lie down in the mountains," they were priests who mixed esoteric Buddhism with Shintō practices, and performed extraordinary ascetic practices far from human populations. They were reputed to have magic abilities and were received with suspicion.
13. *Tengu*: beings with human bodies and the heads of birds that are able to fly, and are considered to be accomplished martial artists. They often enjoyed causing trouble for human beings, especially hypocrites.
14. Hasegawa, *Taiheiki*, 255.
15. Koans are short stories or questions used as objects of meditation given to students of Zen. Responses are not supposed to be "logical,"

but rather to indicate that the student has attained some insight into his own being.

16. Indeed, at the time many artists approached their art as a *michi*—as a whole way of life.

17. In the *Bendōwa*, included in Mizuno, *Shōbōgenzō*, vol. 1.

18. Ibid.

19. In the *Genjo kōan*, included in Mizuno, *Shōbōgenzō*, vol. 1.

20. *Bendōwa*.

21. Scholars differ on the dates of the Muromachi Period. They are variously 1333–1573; 1336–1568; 1392–1573; 1392–1568; and 1473–1568.

22. Zeami is said to have written between sixteen and twenty treatises, but the authorship of some of these is not certain.

23. The name combines the "Kan" of Kan'ami and the "Ze" of Zeami.

24. See page 139.

25. See page 97.

26. See page 97.

27. See page 105.

28. See page 124.

29. Blyth, *Zen and Zen Classics*, vol. 4, 176. This is my own translation of the Chinese text quoted by Blyth.

30. See page 61.

31. See page 134.

32. See either Blyth, *Haiku,* vol. 1, or Gill, *Rise, Ye Sea Slugs!*

風姿花伝

FŪSHIKADEN

The Transmission of Style and the Flower

Zeami

PROLOGUE

If we try to establish the origins of the life-extending art of *sarugaku*, we find that it has been transmitted either from the land of the Buddha (India) or from the Age of the Gods.[1] Yet time has passed, and with the interposition of the ages it no longer lies within our abilities to learn how it first appeared. This art, which recently so many people take pleasure in, dates from the reign of Empress Suiko (592–628), when the regent Prince Shōtoku Taishi ordered Hada no Kōkatsu to create sixty-six pieces of entertainment—either to promote peace in the nation or for public enjoyment—that he called *sarugaku*. Over the generations, writers have used the scenery of nature as a medium for this entertainment. Later, Kōkatsu's descendants passed this art down the line of succession, as priests at either the Kasuga Shrine in Yamato or the Hie Shrine in Ōmi.[2] Thus, the performance of religious rites at both of these shrines thrives to this day.

Thus, when studying the old and admiring the new, you should not treat this elegant art with any trace of distortion. We can perhaps say that someone who understands this art has become accomplished simply because his speech is respectful and his form subtly elegant. The person who wishes to follow this Way should practice no other. The only exception that may quite reasonably apply is the Way of Poetry, which will further enrich this life-extending art by adorning it with elements from nature.

I note here two precepts I have seen and heard from the time of my youth.

- Sensuality, gambling, and heavy drinking are three strict prohibitions stipulated by my father.
- Put strength into your practice, and avoid conceit.

CHAPTER
1

CONCERNING PRACTICE AND AGE

Age Seven[3]

Generally, we consider age seven the time to begin this art. At this age, the child will naturally demonstrate a certain inborn presence. If the child shows a natural talent for dance, movement, chanting, or even for roles showing anger, he should be left to perform them as he will. He should not be taught that "This is good" or "This is bad." If a child is admonished too much, he will lose heart; and if performance begins to be tiresome, he will eventually quit altogether.

A child should only be taught chanting, movement, and dance. He should not be taught role-playing, even if he seems able. He should never participate in the opening play of a performance on a large open stage, but may be allowed to perform in his own style in the third or fourth play of the day, if the time seems right.

From the Age of Twelve or Thirteen

From about this age, a child's voice gradually adapts to the musical scale, and he begins to truly understand the content of Nō. Thus he should now be taught a number of things little by little and in the proper order. Firstly, as he still has the appearance of a child, whatever he does will have grace and subtle elegance. Secondly, his voice will carry well. Because of these two conditions, his weak points will be hidden, and his strong points will seem all the more splendid.

Generally speaking, children should not so much be made to perform the more refined roles in *sarugaku*. This would seem incongruous to those viewing the play, and would impede the child's future progress in Nō. Once he has gained the basic skills, however, he should be allowed anything. Though he may be a child with a child's voice, if he is skillful, what could go awry?

Nevertheless, this Flower is not the true Flower. It is only the Flower of the moment.[4] Therefore, although all practice at this time comes easily, a child's future capabilities should not be determined at this time. During this period, practice should aim at demonstrating the Flower of what comes easily, while emphasizing technique. The child should place utmost importance on certainty in movement, enunciating crisply in the chant, and in securing the patterns of the dance.

From the Age of Seventeen or Eighteen

This period is also of great importance, and practice should not be burdensome. First of all, the actor's voice has changed and he has lost his first Flower. His body, too, becomes awkward and he loses the beautiful elegance of a child. Before this stage, his voice was at its prime, he cut a splendid figure, and he felt at ease. Now, however, the acting methods have suddenly changed, and he loses heart. In the end, if he sees the audience indicating that his performance is poor, he may say that he is embarrassed, and be even further discouraged by one thing after another.

During this period, even if the young actor is pointed out and laughed at, he should pay no attention; at home, though, he should use training methods for his voice appropriate to evening and morning practices, in a pitch natural to him.[5] In his heart he should make a strong vow that this—here and now—is the defining moment in his life, that he will stake his life on Nō, and will not abandon it. He should dedicate all his effort to this. If he were to become disheartened at this point, his performance of Nō would never improve.

Pitch will depend on the nature of the individual voice, but as a rule, the actor at this phase should practice between *ōshiki* and *banshiki*.[6] If the young actor is too concerned about pitch, it may affect his posture, which in turn may possibly cause damage to his voice as he gets older.

The Age of Twenty-four or Twenty-five

The level of artistry that the actor may be able to achieve in his life is determined at this age. Thus, it is a crucial time in practice. By now his voice has already improved and his physique is established. In this Way, there are two blessings:[7] the actor's voice, and his physical appearance. Both are determined at this age. This is the juncture when he begins to exhibit his art and is in the prime of his life. And to this extent, he may stand out in the eyes of others, and observers may praise him as "exceptionally skillful." His Flower at this time is quite novel, and should he even win a competition with men who have been considered masters, he may rise unduly in people's estimation, and may even begin to think of himself as exceptionally skilled. I must repeat again and again, that this attitude is the enemy of the actor. Also, this is not the true Flower. It is the singular Flower of one in his prime, which has transiently impressed observers. A true connoisseur, however, should be able to make this distinction.

Indeed, the Flower of this period is called "the beginner's Flower." It would be shallow of an actor to consider this as his highest point and give himself an air of being accomplished, as this would be a mistaken idea that misses the point of *sarugaku*. Even if he is praised by others and defeats the likes of masters in competitions, he should come to a deep understanding that this singular Flower is only transitory. Further, he should become absolutely determined to master the art of role-playing, to ask detailed questions of those who have grasped the art, and to practice all the more. The mind that understands the Flower of this period to be the true Flower is a mind that is far from the real Flower indeed. What it indicates is merely that the actor is confused about the transitory Flower, and is unaware that he has lost the Flower altogether. This is a matter for those who are called beginners.

You should think this through with great effort. If you have a good understanding of the limits of your own ability, you will not lose that particular Flower for your entire life. But if you think you are more skillful than you actually are, you will lose even the Flower that you formerly possessed. You should understand this well.

The Age of Thirty-four or Thirty-five

During this period, the actor's Nō reaches its absolute height. If he has profoundly understood and mastered the items outlined above, he should be established in his art, acknowledged by the public, and secure in his reputation. But if public approval is wanting, his reputation will not be what he had hoped for. He should then know that no matter how skillful he may be, he is not an actor who has attained the true Flower. If he has not truly mastered his art by now, his abilities will probably decline from the age of forty. He will see evidence of this as time passes. Thus, an actor advances in Nō up to the age of thirty-four or thirty-five, and declines after the age of forty. I must therefore repeatedly state that if an actor does not receive public recognition by this time, he should not think that he has thoroughly mastered Nō.

Here the actor should be all the more cautious. This is the point where he should reflect deeply on how he has reached this point and the means by which he will carry on. Again, if he has not mastered Nō by now, it will be difficult to obtain the public's approval at a later date.

The Age of Forty-four or Forty-five

At this age the methods of performance should change considerably. Even if an actor has received public acclaim and has truly mastered the art, he should have good co-actors with him on stage. Even if his ability does not decline, as the years pass he will inevitably lose the Flower of his appearance and the beauty perceived by others. This may be different for an extraordinarily good-looking man, but a man with only a generally acceptable appearance should not be seen in *sarugaku* without a mask as he gets on in years. Otherwise, he will be lacking in this way.

From this period on, he should not so much perform roles that require fine detail. For the most part he should not overly exert himself, but should act with ease appropriate to his appearance, leaving the performance with Flower to his younger co-actors. Rather, he himself should act more as an associate, and gradually make his own performance more moderate. Even if there are no young co-actors with whom to perform, he should gradually retire from performances requiring extraordinary techniques that may harm his body. In the end, observers will see no Flower there. But if an actor has not lost the Flower by this period, it should indeed be the True Flower.

This being so, an actor who has not lost the Flower as he nears the age of fifty will have received public recognition before the age of forty. Though he may still receive public recognition, this kind of skilled actor will especially know his own abilities well, and will thus use his experience to counsel his younger co-actors. He will further avoid performances that might harm his body and perhaps cause him problems. The mind of the man who knows his own capabilities will thus be the mind of the man who has grasped this art.

Beyond the Age of Fifty

From this age, for the most part there is no better method than "not doing it."[8] A saying has it that "Even Ch'i-lin, when he gets old, can be beaten by a worn-out nag."[9] Thus, even for a true master of Nō, there will be fewer and fewer roles that he can perform, and his merits in those roles will decline. Nevertheless, his Flower should remain.

My father passed away on the nineteenth day of the Fifth Month[10] at the age of fifty-two, but on the fourth day of the same month he performed in honor of the gods and Buddhas at the Sengen Shrine in Suruga.[11] The *sarugaku* that day was splendid, and the spectators of both the upper and lower classes all praised it highly. Generally speaking, most of the roles were given to the young actors, and my father performed the easy parts with restraint and understatement. His performance was charged with such hues, however, that his Flower seemed to have expanded. This is because in Nō, if an actor has truly mastered the Flower, the tree may be old and its branches and leaves few, yet the flowers will remain without falling. This was proof, before my very eyes, of the phrase, "The Flower remaining on a bag of bones."

The above refers to practice over the years.

CHAPTER
2

ROLE-PLAYING

It would be difficult to write about *all* the different aspects of role-playing. Nevertheless, they are essential to the Way, so we must do our best to look into them as well as we can. For the most part, the main intent of this skill is to imitate something in its entirety. However, you should know how to do this with different nuances and degrees according to the situation.

To begin with, imitating the ruler of a country, his great ministers, aspects of the nobility, or the actions of the warrior classes is something beyond our reach, and it is difficult to do them full justice. Still, shouldn't we make inquiries about their speech, investigate their behavior, and listen to their opinions on our performances? Beyond that, all we can do is imitate in detail the occupations of the upper classes and aspects of their elegant arts as well as we can. When it comes to the affairs of rustics and country bumpkins, however, we must not imitate their vulgar ways with too much detail. We should, perhaps, give detailed imitations of those activities of woodcutters, grass cutters, charcoal makers, or salt rakers, all of whom have come to be considered charming. But other than these, we should not imitate the lower classes with too much detail. Furthermore, they should not be performed in front of members of the upper classes, who would likely find them ignoble and uninteresting. You should understand well how to apply this principle.

Women

Generally speaking, it is fitting for young *shite* to play the parts of women. Nevertheless, this is an extraordinarily important role.

First of all, if the actor's appearance is unsightly, it will have no merit whatsoever. It is not easy to observe how court ladies or female attendants dress or act, so in order to imitate them you must ask about these things exhaustively. The way a *kinu*[12] or *hakama*[13] or any other article of clothing is worn is not a matter of the actor's own personal choice. You should research such things. It should be a truly easy matter to perform the roles of simple ordinary women, since you are used to seeing them every day. It is merely a matter of donning a *kinu* or *kosode*,[14] and acting the general essence of a woman with no great to-do. Whether performing an ordinary woman's dance, the *shirabyōshi*[15] of a courtesan, or a madwoman's dance, you should hold either a fan or a spray of flowers in a delicate, feminine manner. Clothing like the *kinu* and *hakama* should be long enough to cover your feet; your hips and knees should be straight, and your body pliant. As for the carriage of your head, if you look upwards it will be perceived as unsightly; if you look down, however, your posture will appear poor when seen from behind. If your head is held with strength, it will not be womanly. Be sure to wear sleeves long enough to conceal the tips of your fingers. A sash or something around the waist should be worn loosely.

This being so, if you take care over your appearance, you should be able to portray womanly aspects well. No matter what sort of role you are playing, your appearance should never be poor; appearance is especially fundamental in women's roles.

Old Men

Playing the role of an old man involves the deepest principles of our Way; as the ultimate level of your ability will be apparent to spectators, it is of the greatest importance.

Generally speaking, there are many leading actors who have delved deeply into Nō, but who have not understood the appearance of an old man. There are those, for example, who have gained praise for their performance of the roles of old men such as woodcutters or salt rakers. Yet this judgment is questionable. And it is not suitable for those who have not acquired considerable skill to portray an elderly noble whether wearing a helmet, everyday aristocratic clothes, a tall black cap, or hunting gear. Such roles are not fitting for actors who have neither put forth great efforts over the years nor yet reached high levels.

Again, if there is no Flower, the portrayal of such a role will likely be of little interest. Many actors merely consider the age of old men and portray them by stooping their hips and knees and shriveling their bodies. Losing their Flower, they just look trite; portrayed like this, the role will rarely be interesting. By and large, you should simply act with as much grace and quiet purpose as possible. In particular, the atmosphere created by the dance of an old man is of utmost importance. The discussion of how to appear old while retaining the Flower is a detailed oral teaching which must be learned. It is just like an old tree blooming with flowers.

The Unmasked Face

This, too, is very important. Generally speaking, this is a matter of our fundamental ordinary self, so it should be an easy matter. Strangely enough, however, if not performed by someone in the higher levels of Nō, an unmasked face can be unwatchable.

First of all it is quite necessary to study each and every subject. However, although it is unreasonable to think that an actor could imitate another person's facial expressions, some actors change their own countenances trying to conjure up some look or another. This is highly unsightly. You should imitate a person's posture and his presence. The facial expression should be your own as much as possible, and you should be as natural as you can.

Madmen

This is the most interesting art in this Way. There are many different kinds of madness, but the actor who has grasped and mastered this one Way should be able to portray them all. Thus I stress again that you must approach this strenuous study in all seriousness. Of the various kinds of spirits that possess others, there are gods, buddhas, wraiths of living persons, and spirits of the dead; and if you study the essence of such spirits, you should be able to communicate them easily. Parents who are searching for children who have become separated from them, women abandoned by their husbands, men who have outlived their wives—people who have become distraught with such preoccupations are quite difficult. Even a good *shite* may not distinguish these mental states, and may act out a single general insanity, but this will give the spectator no impression at all. If, however, you grasp the cause of the madness, make the expression of those feelings your most fundamental and absolute intention, turn the madness into the Flower, and become deranged in your own mind, the impression and visual interest will be established. You should understand that if people are moved to tears with a performance of this nature, your skill has been peerless. You should think this through very carefully within your inmost thoughts.

Generally, it goes without saying that your attire must be fitting to that of a madman. Nevertheless, you should dress according to the circumstances in gorgeous attire, with the understanding that this is someone who has lost his senses. You might also hold a spray of flowers in season.

There is another important point I should mention with regard to playing the role of a mad person. A madman is demented by the deep intention of the possessing spirit, but an actor should never portray a madwoman possessed by an Ashura,[16] the spirit of a warrior, or a demon. The audience will find it inappropriate if you try to express the will of the possessor and portray that anger in a woman's form. Yet if you succeed in portraying the deep impression of the woman's role, you will not do the possessing spirit justice. Likewise you should have the same understanding of a madman possessed by a woman. Avoiding performing Nō of this sort is a secret of this Way, and anyone who writes Nō plays like this does not have this understanding. A writer skillful in this Way would never write such an ill-matched play. This deep understanding is a secret matter.

Furthermore, portraying a madman without a mask requires the deepest understanding of Nō. If you do not give your face the proper air, you will not resemble a madman at all. It will be unsightly if you do not fully understand the role and change the expression on your face accordingly.

The things I am stating here are the deepest principles of role-playing. A beginner acting in major plays of *sarugaku* should consider them very carefully. Imagine the extraordinarily difficult arts of performing without a mask and portraying madmen, make the two into one mind, and apply the Flower to this interesting moment. How very difficult, and what a significant achievement this would be! You must practice this over and over again.

Buddhist Priests

While Buddhist priests are portrayed in this Way, such roles are relatively scarce and so do not require so much practice. For the most part, for gorgeously attired and high-ranking priests, you should do your very best to make dignity and majesty your fundamental concern, and to make a study of elevated noble-mindedness. On the other hand, when it comes to ordinary priests, those who have renounced the world and are engaged in ascetic practices make the pilgrimage their fundamental focus. Thus it is essential that you portray them in as much of a meditative atmosphere as possible. Nevertheless, depending on the theme of the composition, it may take more work than you might think.

Ashuras

This, again, is one of the subjects of Nō. The role is often portrayed, but rarely in an interesting way. They should probably not be performed often. Nevertheless, if the role of a famous warrior such as a Minamoto or Taira[17] is arranged well with representative natural beauty, it should be wonderfully moving. Such plays need to contain an especially spectacular scene. In its essence, the Ashura's insanity tends to take the form of the dance of a demon. However, the play may simply become a vehicle for dance. If there is a section for a dance accompanied by chanting and a hand drum, it should include a few hand movements too. Bows, quivers, and swords are considered appropriate ornaments, but you should investigate thoroughly how they are carried and used. This will enable you to portray the fundamental essence of such characters. You should be extraordinarily careful and guard against turning the role into that of a demon or into a vehicle for dance.

Gods

This type of role resembles that of a demon. The role contains a semblance of anger, so depending on the character of the god portrayed there should be no difficulty in making the portrayal like that of a demon. There is, however, one completely different characteristic. The aesthetic of the dance is correct for a god, while a demon should not communicate though dance at all. In portraying a god, you must demonstrate its character and dignity well, and above all its costume, without which the essence of the god will not be manifested. You must thus decorate your garments and prepare your complete attire appropriately.

Demons

These roles are very much a specialty of Yamato *sarugaku*, and are a matter of consequence to perform. Generally speaking, demons that are revengeful spirits or that possess others are interesting and easy to portray. If the *shite* keeps his eyes intently on the *waki*, gestures with his hands and feet in careful detail, and uses the headgear as a fulcrum for his movements, he will succeed in communicating the role with interest. If you mimic a true demon from hell, it may be frightening but rarely interesting. This role requires a truly inordinate level of skill, and the actors who can make it interesting are, perhaps, rare. From the very first, the fundamental intent of the role should be ferocity and fear. These two qualities, however, can alter the very heart of what is interesting.

All in all, playing demon roles is fraught with difficulties. And it is natural that it becomes less interesting the more the actor attempts to do it well. Instilling fear is the fundamental intent, and fear and interest are as different as black and white. This being so, perhaps we can say that a *shite* able to portray the interesting points of the demon is extraordinarily skillful.

Still, a *shite* wishing to specialize in portraying demons probably does not really understand the Flower. A demon portrayed by a young *shite* may appear to be done well, but in truth will be all the less impressive. Thus, isn't it reasonable to suppose that an actor specializing in portraying demons will probably not make it interesting? This must be studied in detail. The accomplishment of making a demon interesting may be likened to a flower blooming among boulders.

Chinese People

Generally speaking, this is an exceptional matter, so there is no fixed form of practice. The costume, however, is essential. Because all people [Chinese and Japanese] have the same facial characteristics, in this case you should wear a mask of singular design and carry yourself with a presence indicating a difference in origin. This is a role fitting for an experienced leading actor, even though there is no particular method other than making the costume in the Chinese style. Even if the music and the movements truly resemble what is said to be Chinese, this alone is liable to have an uninteresting atmosphere. You should thus have a grasp of one singular Chinese feature.

A singular feature like this, even if just something trifling, is a contrivance that can be carried throughout the entire play. This kind of singular feature is undersirable in other kinds of role-playing. However, since you cannot really imitate a Chinese style, no matter what you do, it is better to change the atmosphere of an ordinary action so that it will be viewed as somehow Chinese by the spectator, and so, indeed, become so.

The above articles cover the main aspects of role-playing. It is difficult to note down in writing any of the details beyond this. Generally speaking, though, if you investigate these articles thoroughly you should be able to grasp the details on your own.

CHAPTER

3

QUESTIONS AND ANSWERS

Question: When starting a performance of *sarugaku*, you first look out at the venue of that day, and know ahead of time its advantages and disadvantages. How can you do this?
Answer: This is a matter of grave concern. Only a person who has truly grasped the Way will know how to do this.

First of all, on observing the location of the play, you should have some premonition as to whether the performance will go well or poorly. This is difficult to explain, but I can give you a general idea. When you perform a play portraying a god to the nobility, the audience will gather together and the gallery will take time to settle down. When it at last settles, the audience will be unable to wait any longer for the performance. At this point the spectators will, as if with one mind, all look toward the mirror room and think, "It's slow in starting." If the actor emerges at precisely that moment and starts his introductory chant, the audience will quickly be moved to the rhythm of the moment. Thus the minds of a great number of people will be in harmony with the actions of the *shite*. If this is felt deeply, the day's performance will go well no matter what.

If, however, you take the presence of the nobility in the audience as your standard, if they should arrive early it would not do to begin the performance late. In such a case, the rest of the audience may not yet be settled down, some may rush in late so that some will be sitting and others standing, and the minds of the spectators will not yet be concentrated on the performance. If this happens, it may not go easily and the play will not be deeply felt. In such a situation, from the beginning of the first play of the day, the actor will have to adjust by behaving more colorfully than he ordinarily would—by putting more strength into his voice, by making his steps slightly higher, by making the atmosphere of his behavior more outstanding to the spectators, and by being more lively altogether. This is for the sake of calming the audience. But even in doing this, it should be done with an atmosphere particularly in keeping with the minds of the nobility. In a case like this, the first play of the day will likely not be performed at its best, regardless of what is done. Nevertheless, it is essential to remain within the sensibilities of the aristocratic element of the audience. Anyhow, nothing will go wrong if the spectators quiet down quickly and feel the play deeply of themselves. An understanding of whether an audience has become interested in the performance or not cannot easily be determined by someone without many years' experience in this Way.

Another point should be mentioned here. The atmosphere for *sarugaku* changes radically at night. If the performance starts late at night, it will be settled and quietly melancholy. The essence of what makes good Nō for the second performance during daylight should thus be employed for the first performance at night. If the *sarugaku* is pervaded with melancholy from the outset, it will remain so throughout the performance. A good performance, however, will be as lively as possible. At night the audience may be rustling about, but with the very first chant it will soon quiet down. Thus, *sarugaku* during the day may become better and better as the performance goes on, but *sarugaku* at night must be good from the start. If the beginning is pervaded with melancholy, it will be very difficult to correct.

I will mention a secret tradition. You should know that all matters are fulfilled at the point where Yin and Yang are in harmony. The *ch'i* of daylight hours is Yang. Thus, making skillful efforts to perform as peacefully as possible is Yin *ch'i*. To produce a Yang performance during the Yin hours is the very heart of harmonizing Yin and Yang. This is the key to being able to perform well, and the heart of making the performance interesting to the audience. So if the nighttime is Yin, you will be performing Nō well when you do so as buoyantly as possible; for it is Yang that makes the mind of man rejoice. This is the fulfillment of harmonizing the Yin of night with Yang *ch'i*. Indeed, there will likely be no points of harmony if Yang is added to Yang, or Yin to Yin, and thus no possibility of fulfillment. How can a performance be interesting without this sense of fulfillment? Furthermore, if at any given moment the venue should become melancholy and lonely for some reason, even during the day, understand this to be a Yin moment and do your best not to sink into it. Although there are moments during daylight hours when Yin *ch'i* is generated, there do not appear to be times at night when Yang *ch'i* appears. This is all relevent when first assessing a venue.

Question: In Nō, how do we determine the *jo, ha,* and *kyū*?[18]

Answer: This is easily done. All things have a *jo*, a *ha*, and a *kyū*, and *sarugaku* is no exception. These are determined by the content of the performance. First, in the opening play of a *sarugaku* performance, the historical source for the performance should be as accurate as possible and performed with grace; but the chanting and movements should be broad and relaxed so that they will be completed smoothly and easily. The first play should be celebratory (*shūgen*, 祝言); no matter how good the first play of a *sarugaku* performance is, it will not be appropriate without a celebratory nature. Even if the Nō is a little patchy, it should cause no embarrassment if it is celebratory. This is because it is the *jo*. The second and third plays should be excellent Nō, reflecting a mature technique and presence. As the final piece of the day is the *kyū*, it should particularly involve vigorous action and difficult technique. Also, the first play of the following day should have a different atmosphere than the first play of the previous day. You should consider the best timing for pieces likely to draw tears, programming them in the middle of the second day's performances.

Question: What about the methods used in *sarugaku* competition?

Answer: This is a crucial point. First, you should have a number of plays in your repertoire, and perform plays with a different atmosphere to those performed by your opponents. This is what I meant in the prologue, when I recommended study of the Way of Poetry. If the actor is not the author of a piece, he cannot perform it simply as he pleases, no matter how skillful he may be. If, however, it is his own work, he can perform both the words and actions his own way. If an actor has some talent for writing Japanese poetry and prose,[19] it should be easy for him to compose *sarugaku*. This is the very life of our Way. But no matter how skillful he may be, an actor with no such talent will resemble a great warrior on the battlefield without his weapons. You should be able to see the quality of a man's skill in the contest. If your opponent performs a colorful Nō, you should change the pattern to something quiet, and perform a play that will have the audience holding its breath. If you perform a different kind of play to that of your opponent, you should not lose, no matter how good his performance may be. And if you perform successfully, your victory will be assured.

Nevertheless, even in proper performances of *sarugaku*, there will be the distinction of high, middling, and low quality. If a piece is taken from a traditional source yet given novel treatment, if it has the quality of a graceful and subtle elegance and yet has points of interest, you may say that it is good Nō. Good plays that are well performed and well received should be considered of the highest quality. A Nō play that is not all that good, but which cannot be criticized as to its choice of source material and is performed well, and is well-received, should be considered middling. A poorly written play that relies on poor sources, yet is well performed through great effort, is low quality.

Question: I have great doubts here. An author may be quite experienced and famous, and yet a young upstart actor may defeat him in competition. This seems strange to me.

Answer: This is precisely what I mentioned before regarding an actor having a temporary Flower before the age of thirty.

When an older leading actor has lost his Flower early on and performs in an old style, someone with a fresh and singular Flower can be victorious. Yet a true judge will be able to see through this, so that it perhaps becomes a contest of judgment between the judges themselves.

Nevertheless, there are reasons for this. An actor who has not lost his Flower even after the age of fifty may not be defeated by a young actor, no matter how good the latter's Flower may be. It is simply that a good and skillful actor is defeated because he has lost his Flower. No matter how famous a tree might be, would we even give it a glance when it is not in bloom? Or would we look at a single-petalled dog-cherry[20] when it blooms before all the others? When you think about an example like this, you understand the principle of how even a temporary Flower may win in a competition.

Thus it is essential to understand that, in this Way, the Flower is the very life of performance, and that older *shite* often make the mistake of not knowing that they have lost their Flower, and are simply relying on their former high reputations. Even though you may be conversant with various types of role-playing, if you do not understand what it is to have the Flower, it will be like collecting grasses and trees when they are not in bloom. The flowers of a thousand grasses and ten thousand trees are all different colors, but to the mind that sees them as interesting, they are all the same: flowers. Although he may know only a few roles, the *shite* who grasps in depth what the Flower is should achieve lasting fame for that one essence. However, if he merely thinks that he has considerable Flower, but does not make efforts to demonstrate it to others, it will be like flowers in the back country or plum trees in thickets, all blooming in vain.

Moreover, even among those who are skillful, there are varying degrees of skill. For example, a *shite* of considerable attainment may have fame, but if he does not put great effort into his Flower, although his skill may be communicated his Flower will not likely last long. A talented actor who puts in great effort, however, will retain his Flower, even though his abilities may deteriorate. And if the Flower itself remains, he should continue to be interesting to the audience for his lifetime. Thus, a *shite* who has truly retained his Flower will not be beaten by another, no matter how youthful the latter may be.

Question: In Nō, actors have their various fortes, and even a remarkably poor actor may be outstandingly skillful in some point or another. Yet the skillful will not imitate the good points of the unskillful. Is this because they feel that it would be unfitting to do so, or that they might not be able to do so?
Answer: In all things there are people who have various fortes and innate talents. A man may have attained a certain rank, but still may be unable to do certain things. Not to study such things may simply be the inclination of a moderately skillful actor. But a truly skillful actor who both

has great abilities and puts forth great efforts would not be lacking skill in any part of his art. Still, not one actor in ten thousand combines these two qualities. This is because people are inflated with pride and do not put in more effort. Even those who are skillfull have weak points. And those who are not have some absolutely strong points. People do not see this, and the actors themselves may not be aware of it. Those who are skillful rely on their fame, are hidden behind their own proficiency, and do not know their own weak points. Those who are unskillful, having made no great effort, not only do not know their weak points, but are also unable to distinguish their own strong points when they do arise. This being so, both the skillful and the unskillful actor should inquire into these matters together. They should know that both ability and effort must be tested to their extremes.

No matter how poor an actor may be, if it is apparent that he has strong points, even a good actor should study those points. This is the best method. An actor may observe such good qualities but be vain enough to think that he should not study them because the other actor is his inferior. With this kind of frivolous mentality, he will not likely ever be aware of his own weak points. This is precisely because his own mentality is not thoroughgoing. Again, a poor actor may perceive the weak points of a good actor and think, "Even a good actor has weak points, so certainly one can imagine that a beginner like me will have as many weak points as I do." If he thinks in this way, takes the matter deeply into account, questions others about these points, and makes great efforts, this process itself will eventually become part of his training, and his capabilities should quickly improve. If, on the other hand, he fails to do this and thinks conceitedly that he himself would hardly commit such mistakes, he will probably not truly know his own strong points. If he does not know his own strong points, he will think that his weak points are strong, too. In this case, the years will go by without any improvement in his Nō. This is precisely the mind of a poor actor. Thus, if even a skillful actor is conceited, his abilities will probably decline. And how much more will this be so for a conceited poor actor? You should think this over and make it your koan: the skillful actor should be the model for the unskillful actor, while the unskillful actor should be the model for the skillful actor. The good actor should take the strong points of a poor actor and make them part of his repertoire. This is a fundamental principle. Even the spectacle of another's weak points should become your model;[21] and how much more so his strong points. This is the meaning of the phrase, "Strengthen your practice, do not be conceited."

Question: How does one understand the distinction in the levels[22] of Nō?
Answer: This is in the eye of the connoisseur, and is easily perceived. For the most part, you raise your level by passing

through the various stages of practice; yet strangely enough, an actor of only ten years old may have an elevated presence at a level that he rises to on his own. Coming to a level on your own without practice, however, is not to your advantage. Reaching a level by first putting effort into practice is the normal state of things. Again, a level achieved by your own innate qualities has *take* (長). What is called *kasa* (かさ) is a different thing altogether. Many people think that *take* and *kasa* are the same, but *kasa* has rather the form of stately authority, and it is said that it embraces all styles of the art. "Level" and *take* are different, too. There are, for example, some who have an innately acquired graceful and subtle elegance. This is what is called "level." Nevertheless, there are actors without this kind of elegance who have *take*. This refers to a level of ability that has not developed a graceful and subtle elegance.

A beginning actor should think about these things. I would emphasize that it is probably unfitting to practice with your mind set on level. Level will not be realized in this way, and whatever you have acquired by practice will also decline. In the end, level and *take* are naturally acquired and for the most part are impossible to grasp. Moreover, as you put effort into your practice and the dust falls away, this level will appear on its own. Practice takes the form of delving into the various aspects of Nō, such as the chant, dance, movement, and role-playing.

You should meditate on this as you would on a koan: perhaps the level of graceful and subtle elegance is something with which one is born. And perhaps the *take* is a matter of effort. You should go over these things deeply in your mind.

Question: How are atmosphere and movement related to text?

Answer: Through very detailed practice. Every sort of movement in Nō is approached in this way, and deportment and posture are the same. Let us say that you guide your mind by entrusting it to the words of the text. If the word "look" appears, you will look at something; for words like "point" or "draw back," you will point or withdraw your hand; for words like "listen" or "make a sound," you will listen with attention. Carry your body in accordance with the various circumstances, and the action will come of itself. First in importance is the body posture; second, the use of the hands; and third, the use of the feet. The movements of the body should be assessed according to the melody of the chant and the artistic effect. This is difficult to perceive in written materials. When the moment comes, you should learn it just by watching.

If the actor performs this practice thoroughly in accordance with the text, the chants and movements should become one. And in the end, this is the very heart of mastery. This is what is referred to as "true skill," and is a secret teaching. The actor who thoroughly and expertly makes the two minds of the chant and the movement one should become skillful beyond compare. This is true Nō.

Again, there are many people who are led astray on the matter of strength and weakness. It is strange that a lack of grace should be considered strength, and that weakness should be judged as a graceful and subtle elegance. There will be *shite* who do not perform in a visibly weak way no matter how you view them. This is strength. An actor who gives a splendid performance regardless of the stage has this graceful and subtle elegance. If you delve thoroughly into this principle and apply it to the text, the chant and the movement will become one, and you will understand the boundaries of strength and elegance. Those who do this will become excellent *shite* on their own.

Question: You often hear the word "wilting" in judgments on Nō. What is this about?

Answer: This is something that cannot be thoroughly expressed in writing, and its aesthetic cannot be easily explained. Properly speaking, however, there is such a thing as the presence of "wilting." This is another aesthetic that depends entirely on the actor's Flower. If you give it careful thought, you may see that it is difficult to achieve either in practice or in acting itself. Perhaps you will understand it if you have thoroughly attained the Flower.

This being so, an actor who has mastered the Flower in one way—even if not broadly in every role—should probably know that moment of wilting, which is said to be even more elevated than the Flower. Without the Flower, the moment of wilting has no meaning, and will likely just be limp. It is the wilting of flowers that is interesting, not the wilting of grasses and trees not in bloom. Thus, if the mastery of the Flower is a matter of great difficulty, the atmosphere of wilting—which is said to be even beyond the Flower—is much more so, and so is even more difficult to explain. An ancient poem reads:

> In the thin mist,
>> flowers on the bamboo fence,
>
> with early morning dew.
>> Who was it who said,
>> in the autumn, evenings are best?[23]

Another reads:

> In this world
>> it is the flower of man's heart
>
> that fades,
>> though this cannot be seen
>> in its hue.[24]

The atmosphere of wilting should be like this. Keep this firmly in mind for rigorous contemplation.

Question: Reviewing the various articles on understanding the Flower in Nō, I can see that it is of the very highest importance and absolutely essential. Yet there is still something I don't understand. How do you *really* come to grasp this Flower?

Answer: This comes through a thorough investigation of the deep principles of this Way. And it is a singular matter of this Way that it is considered to be both of the greatest importance and a secret matter. Now for the most part you have been able to read the various items on practice and role-playing in detail. Matters such as the temporary Flower, the Flower of the voice, and the Flower of a graceful and subtle elegance can be observed by the spectators; they are all Flowers that come forth from technique, and so are like those that bloom, and thus like those that finally fall. In this way, if they do not last for long, their fame in the world will also not endure. As for the true Flower, the cause of its blooming and also of its falling is in the will of the actor. Thus it should last long.

How can you truly understand this principle? Perhaps the hints given in the oral tradition in a separate chapter will help you to understand. At any rate, you are not likely to grasp this by vexatious inquiry. An actor should, from the time he is seven years old, go through the year-by-year items of practice, learn the various types of role-playing, and study them in detail in his heart. He should leave no stone unturned concerning his abilities, and make absolute efforts. After this, he should understand the Flower that he will not lose. The mind that is thorough in all the many kinds of role-playing should be exactly that mind that is the seed of the Flower. If you want to know the Flower, you should first know the seed. The Mind is the Flower; the seed is technique. An ancient worthy[25] said:

> The ground of the Mind holds all seeds;
> the universal rain germinates every one of them.
> When at last you have suddenly awakened to the nature of the flower,
> the fruit of enlightenment will ripen of itself.

I have harbored the matters my late father spoke of deep in my heart in order to remain true to our clan and to honor its art. I have recorded the general points without any thought for society's critics, but rather with the idea that our Way should not fall into disuse. Accordingly, this is absolutely not for the purpose of other people becoming more erudite. It is simply to leave the clan's lessons for our descendants.

The above are Teachings on the Presence of Grace.

Seventh year of Oe[26]
Thirteenth day of the Fourth Month
of the Lunar Calendar

Composed by Saemon Dayū
    Junior Lower Fifth Rank[27]
    Hada[28] no Motokiyo

CHAPTER
4

MATTERS CONCERNING THE GODS

Sarugaku is said to have begun during the Age of the Gods. The story has it that when the Sun Goddess, Amaterasu Omikami, shut herself up in a cave in heaven, the world was plunged into immutable darkness. The myriads of gods gathered together on Heavenly Mount Kagu and performed sacred music and comic dances in order to lure her from the cave. Ama no Uzume no Mikoto came forward and, holding a branch of the *sakaki* tree with a sacred folded-paper offering, raised her voice, ignited lanterns, and stamped her feet. Finally she became possessed and performed both songs and dances. Amaterasu quietly listened to the voices of the gods, then opened up the cave door just a little and the land was filled with light. Now the faces of the gods became bright white. It is said that *sarugaku* had its beginnings from the amusing entertainment on that occasion.[29] The details of this may be found in our oral traditions.

In the land of the Buddha, a wealthy man named Sudatta built the Gion monastery,[30] and at the dedication ceremony, the Buddha delivered a sermon. Devadatta[31] and ten thousand heretics danced and yelled, waved tree branches and bamboo grass with sacred folded papers attached, and made it difficult to continue. The Buddha glanced at Shariputra[32] who, thus filled with the Buddha's powers, quickly arranged a drum and pipe performance at the rear entrance. Then, as sixty-six plays were performed thanks to Ananda's[33] wit, Shariputra's wisdom, and Purna's[34] eloquence, the heretics heard the sound of the pipes and drums, gathered at the rear entrance, and quietly watched. At this time, the Thus Come One[35] continued with the dedication. This was the beginning of our Way in India.

In Japan, during the reign of Emperor Kinmei,[36] a flood occurred in the Hatsuse River in the province of Yamato, and a jar floated down from the upper reaches of that river. A high-ranking court official picked up the jar next to the cedar torii gate at Miwa Shrine. Inside was a jewel-like infant with a tender expression. As this must have been someone descended from Heaven, the noble reported the event to the throne. In the emperor's dream that night, the infant said, "I am the reincarnation of Ch'in Shih Huang Ti[37] of China. I have a karmic relation to the Land of the Rising Sun, and thus have appeared here now." The emperor thought this to be a marvel and summoned the infant to the court. As the child grew to maturity, he was exceptionally intelligent; by the age of fifteen he rose to the rank of minister. Because the Chinese character *ch'in* (秦) is pronounced *hada* in Japanese, he was given the name Hada no Kōkatsu.

Once, during a time of disturbances in the country, Prince Shōtoku put his trust in the ancient examples from the Age of the Gods and from the land of the Buddha, and commanded this Kōkatsu to perform sixty-six pieces of role-playing, while he himself carved the sixty-six masks and gave them to Kōkatsu. Kōkatsu performed the pieces at the Hall for State Ceremonies in the Tachibana Palace. The country was soon brought under control and peace again reigned. Prince Shōtoku handed down these performances for the sake of later generations. He removed the left-hand radical (礻) from the character for divine (神) leaving just the right-hand side of the character (申), which means "to speak" and is pronounced *saru* in Japanese. Combining this with the character used to mean "entertainment" (楽, literally "pleasure"), the performance was given the name *sarugaku*. It thus means "to speak" (申) of "pleasure" (楽), and is also thus distinguished from *kagura* (神楽), or Shintō music and dance.

This same Kōkatsu served successive emperors—Kinmei, Bitatsu, Yōmei, and Sushun, the empress Suiko, and Prince Shōtoku Taishi—handing down this art to his descendants. Then, because wraiths can leave no remains, he set out from

Naniwa Bay in the province of Settsu in a boat carved from a single large tree. Entrusting himself to the wind, he sailed out over the Western Sea and arrived at Shakushi Bay in the province of Harima. When the people of this bay pulled the boat to land, his shape had changed from that of a human being. He began to possess and haunt all the people of the area, and to cause strange omens. The people thereupon began to worship him as a god, and the province prospered. They named him Ōsake Daimyōjin, writing this with the characters meaning "greatly violent."[38] Even today he is astonishingly responsive to prayers, and his true essence is that of Bishamon Tennō.[39] It is said that when Prince Shōtoku Taishi quelled the rebellion of the Moriya,[40] he used this god's power to defeat his enemies.

When the capital was moved to Heian-kyō,[41] Emperor Murakami read the *Sarugaku ennen no ki*, written long before by Prince Shōtoku. This document stated that *sarugaku* had originated in the Age of the Gods, and then the land of the Buddha; that it had then been transmitted through the Trans-Oxus, China, and finally to Japan; and that its "crazy words and extravagant language"[42] served to praise the Buddha, to protect Japan's karmic relation with his turning the Wheel of the Law, to dispel evil influences, and to invite prosperity. Thus, if *sarugaku* were performed, the country would be calm, the people would be at peace, and all would enjoy longevity. In accordance with what Prince Shōtoku had written down, Emperor Murakami felt that *sarugaku* would serve as prayers for the nation. About this time there was a man by the name of Hada no Ujiyasu, a distant descendant of Kōkatsu—who had inherited the art of *sarugaku*—and he performed the sixty-six plays in the Hall for State Ceremonies. At the same time there was a man by the name of Ki no Go no Kami, who was full of wit and intelligence. He was the husband of Ujiyasu's younger sister, and performed *sarugaku* along with him.

Later, Ujiyasu felt that it was difficult to perform the sixty-six plays in one day, and established three plays from among them as standard: the Inatsumi Okina with the *okina*[43] mask, the Yonatsumi Okina, and the Chichi no Jō. In the present period, these are what are known as the "Three Special Plays," and represent the Three Bodies of the Buddha: the Dharmakaya, the Sambhogakaya, and the Nirmanakaya.[44] The oral tradition of the Three Special Plays will be recorded in a separate chapter. There are twenty-nine generations of descendants from Hada Ujiyasu, to Kōtaro, to Konparu of the current Enman-i troupe of Yamato Province. Ujiyasu likewise handed down three things to this clan: a demon mask carved by Prince Shōtoku, a painting of the Great God of the Kasuga Shrine, and a skeletal relic of the Buddha.

Nowadays, while the *Yuima-e*[45] service is conducted in the lecture hall at Kōfukuji Temple in the Southern Capital (Nara), longevity dances are performed in the refectory. These are intended to soothe heretics and to pacify those afflicted with demons. During this time, a lecture on the Yuima Sutra is also given in front of the refectory. Thus, the Yuima dances are based on the time-honored example of the dedication of the Gion monastery. Religious observances[46] are also performed at Kasuga Kōfukuji in Yamato Province on the second and fifth days of the Second Month. Four *sarugaku* troupes perform these, which mark the first of the religious events that will be celebrated throughout the year. These performances constitute prayers for the tranquility of the country. The following troupes perform:

- Four *sarugaku* troupes follow the Shintō ceremonies in Kasuga: Tobi, Yūzaki, Sakado, and Enman-i.
- Three *sarugaku* troupes follow the Shintō ceremonies at Hie in Ōmi: Yamashina, Shimosaka, and Hie.
- Two Shushi troupes in Ise, and the current incantatory Shushi troupe.
- Three *sarugaku* troupes that participate in the New Year's ceremonies at Hosshōji Temple: Shinza, Honza, and Hōjōji. These troupes likewise follow the Shintō ceremonies at Shiga Sumiyoshi.

CHAPTER
5

PRAISING THE DEEPEST PRINCIPLES

I hesitate to expose these secret teachings to the eyes of those generally outside of our art, and am writing them down here rather as precepts for our descendants. Nevertheless, I do have one basic intention. When I look at people who practice these days, I see that they make light of our art, follow practices outside of our own Way, and even when reaching a high level in the art, imbue themselves with a single night's enlightened performance or momentary fame. I can only lament that they have forgotten the wellspring of our art and lost its current, and that the true Way is perhaps already in decline. If you take care to follow the Way, place great importance in the art, and leave your own self-interest to one side, however, you should be able to grasp the grace of its character. In our art especially, though its ancient customs are handed down from generation to generation, there are on occasion performances that are successful due to the actors' individual strengths, and these things are difficult to put into words. But in the continuation of our style, the Flower is passed down from mind to mind,[47] and so I have named this book the *Fūshikaden*, or "The Transmission of Style and the Flower."

Generally speaking, our Way is different from the styles of the Yamato and Ōmi schools. In Ōmi, they promote a graceful and subtle elegance while placing secondary importance on role-playing, and they make an aesthetic sense their fundamental. In Yamato, role-playing is promoted first and all roles are exhaustively studied, but an atmosphere of a graceful and subtle elegance is also sought. Nevertheless, no matter what kind of style is assumed, the truly skillful actor should allow for no openings or lapses in concentration. The actor who aims to perform only one of these styles is one whose technique will never reflect a true grasp of the essence of the art.

Accordingly, many have come to understand the Yamato style as one that makes role-playing or the storyline its fundamental point. They think that its actors adorn themselves with *take*, emphasizing wrathful performances and the like. It is a fact that such acting is given great attention, but when my late father was at the height of his fame, it was particularly his grasp of the atmosphere of the plays *Shizuka ga mai* and *Saga no dainenbutsu no onnagurui* that won him praise and fame everywhere. These facts are not hidden from the world. In these performances, his display of a graceful and subtle elegance was supreme.

Many people have come to think that the acting of *dengaku*[48] is quite different from our own, and that the audience cannot compare its style to ours. Yet Itchū of the Honza troupe, reputed to be the true sage of the *dengaku* Way these days, performs particulary the roles of gods and demons, and of wrathful beings, among all those he thoroughly practices. I have heard that his performances are flawless, and for that matter, my late father said quite plainly that Itchū's performances were always instructive for his own style.

It is simply a fact, then, that many actors—whether due to a contentious attitude or a lack of understanding—learn only one style, do not know a full range, and dislike the style of other schools. Yet this is not a true dislike, and merely reflects their shallow willfulness. Because of this attitude, an actor may gain a reputation for one particular style for a short time, but his Flower will not last long, and he will not have the confidence of the public. A master of the art who has achieved public acclaim will make an interesting performance regardless of which style he employs. Every style and fundamental form has its own character, but what makes them interesting should be common to all of them. What makes the spectator see the performance as interesting will be the Flower. And this has not been lacking in the performances of the Yamato and Ōmi schools, or in *dengaku*. If an actor does not have this thing that "has not been lacking," he will not likely be recognized by the public.

There are also actors who may not have delved deeply into all the different kinds of role-playing. However, if a skillful man is well-learned in seventy to eighty percent of them, makes the styles he has understood into the fundamental repertoire of his own troupe, and puts forth great efforts, he should enjoy public acclaim. Nevertheless, if his performances have serious weaknesses, he is not likely to receive the praise of his audiences either in the city or the countryside, or from either high or low classes.

Generally speaking, there are many ways of gaining fame in Nō. It will be difficult for a skillful actor to satisfy people of poor judgment, and a poor actor will not truly be worthy of the attention of people with good judgment. This should not be surprising. A skillful actor may not please people of poor judgment because the eyes of such people are not up to the task. Nevertheless, a truly skillful actor who has grasped the art and continually makes great efforts should have some way of performing that will also interest people of poor judgment. An actor who has done everything in his power and so has gained proficiency is said to be a man who has delved deeply into the Flower. Thus, no matter what his age, an actor who has reached this level will never be inferior to a younger actor with Flower. He will not only have the confidence of the aristocrats in Kyoto, but should be found equally interesting in faraway provinces and the countryside. An actor who has truly grasped the results of such efforts will be able to perform in the style of Yamato or Ōmi, or even in the style of *dengaku*, in accordance with people's preferences and wishes. No matter what style he chooses, his skill should pervade them all. It is in order to reveal the fundamental meaning of such discretion that I have written the *Fūshikaden*.

Having said this, it is the very life of Nō never to make light of the fundamental principles of the style you follow. If you did so, you would be a weak actor. It is precisely by going deeply into the essential forms of your own style that you will be able to know a broad range of styles. The actor who thinks he should know a broad range of styles and thereby ignores his own, will not only fail to have a presence of his own, but will most likely know even less about other styles. In this way his Nō will be weak and his Flower will not last for long. A Flower that does not last long is probably equivalent to not knowing other styles. Thus, in the section on questions and answers I wrote that after you have made extraordinary efforts and left no stone unturned in the various kinds of role-playing, you should know that your Flower will not fade.

With regard to secret matters, it is said that the origin of the art of Nō is to soothe the minds of the people, and to move the sensibilities of both the high and the low equally. This is the very basis for a long life, happiness, and prosperity, and is further the means to extend one's longevity. All of the arts promote these benefits to an astonishing degree. Our art in particular, especially when taken to its highest levels, will earn you the confidence of the entire country and leave your name to posterity. This *is* long life, happiness, and prosperity.

Nevertheless, there is something you should understand. When a performance by an actor of masterful *take*[49] and a certain level of the art is observed by people with real ability and knowledge, the two sides are quite suited to each other, and there is no problem. But for the most part, to the humble eye of the uninformed provincial or country bumpkin, a style of *take* and a high level of the art is beyond its ability to appreciate. What should be done in such a case?

In this art, the foundation of the happiness and prosperity of a troupe should rest on the love and respect of the people. Thus, if only styles that are far beyond the audience's reach are performed, their praise will surely wane. For this reason, you should not forget the way you were as a beginner and, according to the time and place, should perform with the simplicity of the observer in mind. This is true long life and happiness. There are actors who can perform without criticism at aristocratic venues, mountain temples, the countryside, the far-off provinces, and at the festivals of every kind of shrine, and when you really look deeply at the ways of the world, these are the men who perhaps can be said to be skillful in promoting longevity and happiness. No matter how skillful an actor may be, it would be difficult to label him as promoting longevity if he lacks the love and respect of the people. In this light, my late father himself portrayed his art by understanding the mentality of the audience—even in the countryside or some remote country village—and by placing great importance on their customs and morals.

Even explained in this way, the beginner should not lose heart or wonder just how deeply he might be able to delve into the subject. He should take the items discussed here to the very core of his heart, work through their principles one by one, and, with discretion, look into his own portion of strength. In this way, he should make some achievements. Generally speaking, what I have been describing should be more readily grasped by the skilled actor than by the beginner. It is lamentable that actors who have achived a certain level of skill are obsessed with their own position and bewitched by their own fame. Many such men lack proper understanding and thus the gift of longevity, and this is due entirely to their fame. Even with some understanding, they will lack achievement and remain unfulfilled. Having both understanding and masterful achievements, however, is like having both the Flower and the seed. Even an actor who has a grasp of the art and the confidence of the public may temporarily fall out of favor through some karmic situation beyond his control. But if he does not lose the Flower and is praised in the countryside and far provinces, he should not suddenly be cut off from the Way. And if the Way is not cut off, there should come a time when he will once again meet successfully with the public.

I have mentioned the importance of the principle of longevity, happiness, and prosperity. If you get caught up in the ways of the world and are consumed by greed, it will be the first cause of the decline of the Way. If you take great care in these things for the sake of the Way, you should have a long life, happiness, and prosperity. Nevertheless, if you do so merely for the sake of a long life, happiness, and prosperity, the Way will surely decline. And if the Way declines, so too will longevity and happiness of their own accord. You should take great care to live honestly and with clarity; this will be the cause of revealing the mysterious Flower of ten thousand virtues to the entire world.

What I have noted in the *Fūshikaden*—beginning with the practice appropriate to age, to these present notes—do not originate from any resourcefulness of my own. From the time I was quite young, I received the influence and assistance of my late father. I have written down here exactly what I have seen with my eyes and heard with my ears in the way that they came to me in the twenty years since I became an adult. This is for the sake of the Way and for the sake of my clan, and in no way for any benefit of my own.

Ninth year of Oe[50]
Second day of Late Spring
Written in haste by Zea

CHAPTER
6

CULTIVATING THE FLOWER

Writing the texts of Nō is the very life of this Way. Even without the strength of talent and learning, good Nō can be developed just by using skill. General points regarding construction and style can be read in the section on *jo*, *ha*, and *kyū*.[51]

For the opening play, especially, you should base your story on something that you have accurately researched, so that the audience may immediately identify the story from the opening words of the actor. Though you need not labor too much to create a detailed atmosphere, the general aesthetic should be displayed in a gentle, easy tone that nevertheless makes a colorful flourish at the outset. Subsequent plays, on the other hand, should be written with as much detailed attention to the words and the atmosphere as possible. For the most part, if the subject of a play concerns a famous location or a site of historic interest, you should add a Japanese or Chinese poem connected with the spot to provide words that will be familiar to the audience. You should not write in such essential words, however, in places where the *shite*'s words and presence do not apply. At any rate, the audience will not be raptly attentive to what they see and hear unless the actor is skillful. The words and actions of the *shite* will arouse strong feelings in the audience if they are both interesting and are visually striking or allude to something they are familiar with. This is of major importance for the writer of Nō.

A writer should only select words from Japanese and Chinese poems that have charm, and that will be quickly understood. If an actor can bring such charm-filled words and his gestures together harmoniously, his carriage will of itself somehow possess a presence of a graceful and subtle elegance. Rough and stiff words will not be in harmony with gestures, but on the other hand the very incomprehensibility of such words may be fitting to the character who is at the very heart of the story. This should be understood according to whether the character is Chinese or Japanese. Simply speaking, vulgar and rude words make bad Nō.

We can say, then, that good Nō consists of a play based on accurately researched material, an extraordinary atmosphere, a vital or climactic moment, and an aesthetic of graceful and subtle elegance. This will be considered the ideal. Even when a play does not have an extraordinary atmosphere, if there is nothing complicated about it and it runs smoothly, with interesting moments, it may be considered the second best. These are the general rules. If a play has just one point where a skillful actor can demonstrate presence, it will be of interest. When performing a play many times, or perhaps day after day, even a bad play will be perceived as interesting if some embellishment or novelty is added repeatedly. Thus, Nō depends on timing and circumstance. You should not discard inferior Nō indiscriminately; it should be a matter of the leading actor's circumspection.

There is, however, something you must understand. There are some Nō plays that should absolutely not be performed. You may think that any kind of role may be performed, but plays involving elderly nuns, old women, or elderly priests should not be performed if the protagonists are portrayed as angry or insane. Likewise, the role of an angry person cannot be performed with graceful and subtle elegance. This would truly be a false and warped representation of Nō. I have spoken about the heart of this matter in chapter two, when discussing roles of madness.

Again, in all things, there will likely be no attainment without a grasp of balance and proportion. When a play with a good foundation is performed successfully by a skillful actor, it can be said to have balance and proportion. People have become accustomed to thinking that if a good play is performed by a skillful actor, there will be no reason for it to be unsuccessful. Strangely, though, some are not successful at all. Spectators with good judgment will see through the situation and will know enough not to blame the actor, but most people will think that neither the actor nor the play are any good. We must make some effort, then, to understand how a good play with a skillful actor might be performed unsuccessfully. I would wonder whether there was not some lack of harmony between Yin and Yang at that moment, or whether perhaps not enough effort had been put into the actor's Flower. There is still some doubt in my mind about this.

There is a matter that the writer of Nō should think through with care. There are many plays based entirely on a tranquil story line and accompaniment, and others based strictly on dance and action. Such plays can be easily written, but are somewhat unbalanced. In good Nō, however, gestures and actions should be based on the chanting. This is extremely important; it is what creates a feeling of true charm. A play should be written with interesting words that can be readily understood when heard, are well connected to the melody, and sequence beautifully as the words change one into another. Special care should be taken that the vital moment or climax contains a strong aesthetic sense. Balance and proportion in these main elements will create a strong impression in the audience as a whole.

There is a further matter that you should grasp in detail.

An actor who expects the chanting to follow his movements is in the position of a beginner. This is because for an actor with many years experience, movement is given life by the chanting. Chanting is what is heard, presence is what is seen. It is a principle in all things that we make the fundamental our Way, and thus create the myriad aspects of our lives. It is the word that manifests the fundamental. Thus, the chant is the substance, and the aesthetic appearance is the function. In this way, the natural order is that action is born from chanting; chanting in accordance with the actions is the inverse. In all Ways, in all things, the natural order comes first, not the inverse order. To state the matter emphatically, you must create a colorful atmosphere by following the words of the chants. This is the practice of making the chanting and the actions one mind.

In this regard, there is still another great effort that must be made when writing Nō. In order to have the action arise from the chanting, a play must be written with the acting or presence as its fundamental objective. When the words are chanted, a certain presence should then come forth of itself. When you write, therefore, put action or presence at the fore, but take great care over the melody of the chant. When the time comes for the actual performance, though, put the chanting to the fore. If you are very careful in this way, over many years of experience the chant will become the acting, the dance will become the music, and you should become an accomplished master for whom all chanting and acting will become one mind. This is how you gain fame as a writer of Nō.

In Nō, you should understand the difference between performances that are strong and those that are rough, and between performances that have a graceful and subtle elegance and those that are simply weak. You may think this is an easy matter, but many actors give weak or rough performances because they do not truly understand this point. First of all, you must understand that in any kind of role-playing there will be rough or weak points in an unreal fabrication.[52] If your effort at this critical point is haphazard, you may become confused. You must reflect deeply and critically on this from the bottom of your heart.

First, it is an unreal fabrication to portray something that should be weak in a strong way, and this is called "rough." But it is strong rather than rough to portray something that should be strong in a strong way. Any attempt to portray something that should be strong with graceful and subtle elegance will bear no likeness to role-playing; it will have no such elegance and will simply be weak. To this extent then, simply entrust the performance to role-playing: if you enter the role completely and use no unreal fabrication, the performance should be neither rough nor weak. Note that even if the role is meant to be strong, if you go too far with your performance, it will end up being especially rough. Likewise if you try to create an atmosphere of graceful and subtle elegance with too much delicacy, it will be especially weak.

However, if you understand there to be a separate existence for this kind of elegance and strength, you will be missing the point. Both are the essences of the objects portrayed. In the case of human beings, for example, court ladies, their attendants, women of pleasure, beautiful women, and good-looking men are like the different kinds of flowers among the grasses and trees, and as such are objects with forms of graceful and subtle elegance. Warriors, rough barbarians, demons, and gods, on the other hand, are like the pines and cedars in the world of plants, and perhaps they can be said to be objects of strength. In fully portraying these many and varied types, a role of graceful and subtle elegance will have that elegance, and a role of strength will of itself be strong. But if you do not quite grasp this distinction, and only understand what it is to *try* at this elegance, your role-playing will look foolish and be altogether unfitting. The man who does not realize that his performance is unfitting, but only thinks that "This is really a graceful and subtle elegance!" will be a weak actor. If an actor skillfully performs the role of someone like a woman of pleasure or a good-looking man, his portrayal should have subtle elegance of itself. He should only think about portraying that particular role. And if he portrays a role of strength well, his performance should of itself be strong.

However, here is something you should understand. By necessity, our Way is an art that makes the viewer its very foundation; and the viewers' likes and conventions vary with the generations. Thus, when performing a strong role before an audience that prefers a graceful and subtle elegance, depart from the true role-playing a little in the direction of elegance. This is a device that the writer should also understand. As much as possible, the character who displays such elegance should be carefully written into a *sarugaku* storyline as being graceful, and his mentality and words should especially reflect this. If the actor identifies himself completely with this role, he will naturally be perceived as an actor with a graceful and subtle elegance. If you have a complete understanding of the principle of this quality, you should also understand performances requiring strength. If you are thus able to portray every different kind of role, you will not be seen as unreliable by others. In this there is strength.

There are also words that have very faint reverberations: words like "to flutter," "to lie down," "to turn back," or "to approach" are all delicate and seem to give some lingering impressions of themselves. "To fall," "to collapse," "to crush," and "to tumble down" all have strong reverberations and should be exercised with strength. In this sense, there is no difference between "strength" and "a graceful and subtle elegance": they simply imply good role-playing, while "weak" and "rough" indicate something wide of the mark. It would thus be a mistake for the writer—regardless of the character being portrayed—to use rough words, unexpected terms in Sanskrit, or Chinese pronunciations in places where he is seeking out a content of lingering subtle elegance, such as in the opening verse, in high-pitched chanting, or in a Japanese poem. Certainly the aesthetics of the role combined with such words will make the character altogether unbecoming. A skillful actor, however, will understand this contradiction, make a supreme effort, and act the part in a gentle way. This is what makes a great actor. The writer's mistakes should not be ignored. On the other hand, it would be altogether absurd if the writer were to create the work in full understanding of these conditions, only to have the actor ignore them. This is the way things are.

There is also Nō that should be performed in a broad style, without being overly scrupulous about the details of the words or the storyline. Such Nō should be acted straightforwardly, with the dance, chanting and gestures performed smoothly and gently. To pay attention to fine detail in such plays is poor technique. You should understand that such oversight will lead to the decline of Nō. It would likewise be incompetent not to seek fine words and lingering charm in a play that includes a storyline and climax. In straightforward Nō, even when the chanted words of a character endowed with a graceful and subtle elegance are overly rigid, as long as the framework of the chant is kept steady all should be well. You should understand that this is a fundamental aspect of Nō. I must therefore repeat again and again that the things that I have discussed here should be thoroughly investigated and applied broadly. To do otherwise is outside our clan's teachings on Nō.

To determine if a Nō play is good or bad, you should understand whether or not it is fitting to the skill of the actor. Nō plays that do not seek beautiful words or a presence of subtle elegance and require rather a broad performance, yet are nevertheless created on authoratitive sources, are Nō of high quality. Such plays do not need to be viewed with great attention to detail, and thus even a fairly skilled actor may not succeed in the role. Yet even if the actor is entirely suitable and absolutely peerless in skill, he may not carry the role off well if the spectators do not have good judgment and the venue is not a large one. In such a case, the "level" of the Nō, the skill of the actor, the judgment of the audience, the venue, and the moment must all be right, or it will likely not be successful.

Nō of lesser quality will not place so much importance on authoritative sources, but will go into minute detail concerning an atmosphere of graceful and subtle elegance. Such plays are fitting for beginning actors. Suitable venues are outdoor locations, remote country shrines, and courtyards at night. A great number of spectators and actors, too, are confused by these plays. Although they may appear interesting in natural settings, in the countryside, or in small courtyards, they may prove to be astonishingly poor Nō when performed somewhere like a large regal venue, a noble's courtyard, or even in a sponsored public performance. In such instances, the actor's reputation may suffer, and he may lose face. This being so, unless an actor can perform indiscriminately with any work at any location—not just the ones mentioned here—he cannot be said to have mastered a skill of the highest Flower. But if he *has* reached a skill that is suitable for any setting, no more can be done.

Some actors seem to be skillful in technique, but do not really understand the essence of Nō, while others have an understanding of the essence of Nō that exceeds their skills. The former may show technical skill in a performance at a noble's mansion or some large venue, but does something amiss and makes a mistake in the performance itself that is due to his lack of understanding of Nō. Also, a less-skilled actor who knows only a few plays well—in other words, a beginner—may be able to produce his Flower in some august venue, receive the praise of everyone, and do nothing unworthy. This is probably because his knowledge of Nō exceeds his skills. Accordingly, there are various opinions about these two types of actors. However, an actor who is able to perform well at a noble's manor or a large venue will have the lasting fame, even though he may feel more lacking in technique than an actor who is more skillful than knowledgeable of Nō.

Nevertheless, an actor who truly understands Nō will perhaps be superior at establishing and supporting a troupe of his own.

An actor who understands Nō will also know where his own skills are lacking. At any great event of Nō, therefore, he will take his own weaknesses into consideration and put the styles he has grasped well to the fore. If he does this well, he should always receive the praise of his audience. As for his weak points, he should work on them at small venues and at performances in out-of-the-way places. If he disciplines himself in this way, he will gradually and naturally improve in proportion to his efforts to correct himself. In this way, he will gradually add to the volume of his capabilities, shed his blemishes; and eventually, when he has fame, a troupe, and prosperity, his Flower will definitely remain even through the advance of years. This is because he understood Nō from the time he was a beginner. If you thoroughly consider all the problems and koans of Nō with this understanding mind, you will understand the seed of the Flower.

Although the comparative virtues of these two types will very likely be discussed widely and with great interest, each should perhaps solve this conflict on his own.

The above concerns the cultivation of the Flower. It should not be shown to anyone other than those committed to this art.

Zea

CHAPTER
7

ADDITIONAL ORAL TRADITIONS

In the oral tradition, in order to understand the Flower you should first observe a flower blooming in nature, and then understand this as a metaphor for the principle of the Flower in all things.

First then, as with all the myriad trees and grasses, flowers bloom with the time and season. Thus, when a flower's time has come to bloom, we praise it as something unique. In *sarugaku*, too, what the audience understands as unique will be exactly what he finds to be interesting. The Flower, that which is interesting, and that which is unique—these three are the same at the heart of the matter. Yet what flower does not fall, but remains forever on the branch? It is precisely because the flower does fall that it is so unique when it blooms. To understand why Nō does not have one single underlying style or presence, you must first understand flowers. Without one underlying acting style, many may come and go, and all will have that sense of the unique.

There is, however, a very important detail here. You should never introduce an unknown style just because you consider it to be unique. You should discipline yourself completely in all of the items found in the *Fūshikaden*, and then when you perform *sarugaku*, carry it through by being faithful in the usages of the different roles. To speak of flowers, even in the world of grasses and trees, it would be a unique flower indeed that bloomed out of its season or time. Likewise, if you have thoroughly mastered all of the things there are to learn and remember, you will have grasped what is preferred at various times. You will then be able to perform a style according to what people will enjoy at that particular moment, and for them it will be just like looking at flowers blooming in their season. Flowers that bloom this year are from the seeds of those that bloomed a year ago. In Nō, too, you may produce an atmosphere that has been seen before, but if you have thoroughly mastered all of the many kinds of roles, a long time will have elapsed between your performances of a particular role. If a performance has not been seen for a long time, it will once again be perceived as being unique.

Yet people have various predilections, and the chanting, movement, and role-playing are different and change from place to place, so you cannot merely set aside any particular style. The actor who exhaustively masters the different methods of role-playing will thus be like a man who carries the seeds of flowers for every season—from the plum blossom of early spring to the chrysanthemum in the fall. He should therefore be able to produce any type of Flower according to the people's desires or to the season. If he does not master all the various roles, however, he will lose that Flower, depending on the moment. For example, there comes a time when the spring flowers have wilted and the summer grasses are flowering, and an actor who has only grasped the atmosphere of the spring flowers will merely affect the long-gone flowers of spring and ignore the flowers of the summer grasses. So how can his Flower be fitting to the season? Your understanding should be along these lines. The Flower is a unique Flower only in the mind of the spectator. Thus, the oral tradition refers to what was written in the question and answer section of this book: after you have delved deeply into the many kinds of role-playing and made exhaustive efforts, you should understand what it is to not lose the Flower. This being so, the Flower is not something special in itself. The Flower consists of being thorough in the various kinds of role-playing, making great efforts, and understanding the perception of the unique. This is what I meant when I wrote, "The Flower is the Mind; the seed is technique."[53]

In the section on performing demon roles I wrote, "The man who wishes to perform only demons well will probably not understand the interesting points of demons." Exhaustively studying the various kinds of role-playing and portraying a demon uniquely will be interesting to the extent that the unique points are the Flower. An actor may consider himself skillful at the portrayal of demons and exclude all other roles. Indeed, he may be observed to portray demons well. But the very heart of the matter may not be unique, so that there will be no real Flower in the performance. This is what I was referring to when I said it was "like a flower blooming among boulders."[54] Generally, the only style for portraying demons is with strength, being frightening and terrifying the spectators. This is the rock. The Flower is when an actor who knows all the styles and is known for being especially good at graceful and subtle elegance astonishes the audience with his performance of a demon. The points observed as being unique will be the Flower. An actor who only portrays demons, however, is simply the rock; he does not have the Flower.

The oral traditions say that the chanting, the dance, the action, the gestures, and the presence are all of the same mind. Spectators may think that a performance is no different than before because the action and the chanting are as usual. At this juncture, however, the actor should not base his performance on precedent, even though the gestures are the same. Rather, he should take just a little more care with the atmosphere of the role in his heart of hearts. Then, although the chanting is the same as before, he should concentrate his efforts, and carefully add color to the music and his delivery. He must place great importance on this in his mind, and concentrate as he never has before. If the actor uses these techniques, the spectators will find his performances much more interesting than usual, and he will receive critical acclaim. And will this not be because the spectators have felt something unique in their minds?

This being the case, a skillful performance can be distinctly interesting, even if the chanting and the actions are the same. A poor performance will not be thought of as unique because it will have been done in a bland textbook way, just as the actor learned it. Though a chant may be performed with the same old composition, a skillful actor will have a deep understanding of the melody, and the melody may be said to be the Flower that is transcendent of the composition itself. If he makes unparalled efforts in these mysteries, that same skillful actor, within his same Flower, will come to understand that Flower even more. Generally speaking, the chant is fixed within the composition, but the melody belongs to the skilled actor. In the dance, too, the gestures are based on certain practices, but the presence belongs to the skilled actor.

At a certain level, role-playing is no longer a matter of imitation. When you have made an exhaustive study of role-playing, and have truly entered into and become the subject of the role, your mind will no longer think, "I will imitate this."

Thus, if you take special care with the true charm of a performance, will you not have the Flower? In performing the role of an old man, for example, the mind of a skilled actor who has truly grasped the role will only be like that of the old man: he will be an amateur who has costumed himself and who is determined to dance or play music for an artistic demonstration or religious festival. As the actor himself becomes the old man at his very foundation, he should have no thoughts of imitating him. He should only take great care with the true character of that role at that very moment during his dance.

Furthermore, in the oral traditions on the Flower and the appearance of an old man, it states that it is of utmost importance not to think of being like an old man in his behavior. Certainly, for ordinary dance and movements, an actor would totally conform to the rhythm of the music; that is, the stamping of his feet, the extension or withdrawal of his hand, his gestures, and his appearance in general would be in accord with the rhythm. Once becoming an old man, however, in keeping up with the rhythm, the actor will move his feet and extend and withdraw his hands slightly behind the lead of the large drum, the chant, and the small drum. Generally, all of his gestures and presence will be performed in a way to be a little behind the rhythm. This understanding is the fundamental essence of an old man. Carry this application deep in your heart; other than this, just act as colorfully as possible in an everyday manner. When you think about it, an old man would like to do everything just as he did as a youth. Nevertheless, his body inevitably feels heavy, his ears are failing and, although his mind races ahead, physically he cannot keep up. Understanding this principle is the real truth of roleplaying. The actor's techniques should be like the old man's hopes, and he should perform them as a young man. Isn't this how the old man would act, imitating the young with envy? Yet no matter how much an old man tries to make his actions like those of the young, he will be slightly behind in the rhythm; his body lacks the strength, and there is nothing he can do about it. An old man acting like a youth contains the principle of the unique. It is like having flowers bloom on an old tree.

An actor should understand all the various styles of Nō. An actor who has a grasp of all the styles may perform the same repertoire time after time, and although one set of plays may extend over a long period, the audience will still have a sense of the unique. An actor who has grasped all the styles will insert his own inventions and devices, giving the performances a hundred nuances. In order to perform the entire repertoire within a period of three to five years, you should have some plan to keep the performances fluid and unique. This will give you a great sense of spiritual peace. You should, moreover, be mindful of the changing seasons and times within a single year. For a *sarugaku* performance that lasts a number of days—not to speak of one that lasts only a single day—you must add color to the atmosphere of a play, and also to the various plays themselves according to the circumstances. In this way, you will quite naturally take care of everything, from the grandest venues to the smallest details, and you should not lose your Flower for your entire life.

It is also said that more than knowing all the various styles, it is important that you should not forget the Flower you gained in previous years. What is this "Flower obtained in previous years?" Let me illustrate this. The "various styles" means all of the different kinds of role-playing. "Obtained in previous years" means the forms and styles you used when young, the techniques you used as a beginner, the full range of techniques you applied in your thirties, and the presence you have gained as an older actor. With all of these styles and deep understandings you have made a presence for yourself over the years, and they are now carried within your art at the present moment. At times appearing as a child or a youth, at times giving the impression of an actor in the prime of life, yet at times like an actor of profound and refined achievements: an actor should perform in such a way that he does not appear always as the same man. This is the principle of harboring in the present the art obtained from childhood to old age. This is what is said to be "the Flower gained in many previous years."

However, no actors having reached such a level have been

seen or heard of from times long past down to our present age. Nevertheless I believe I have heard that my late father was especially capable of performing an accomplished and refined Nō in the style of his youth. From the time he had passed the age of forty, I was accustomed to watching him and had no doubts about his abilities at all. When he performed the play *Jinen-koji* on an elevated dais, there were reports that the spectators thought he appeared to be sixteen or seventeen years old. As this is truly what people said—and, indeed, how he appeared to me—I feel that he was perhaps an accomplished man who had approached this level to a great degree. Otherwise I have never seen or heard of any actor who was able to grasp a style in his youth that he might use throughout his life and, upon reaching old age, retain those styles he had obtained when he was young.

Thus, an actor should not forget the various things he has learned of the art of Nō from the time he was a beginner, but should apply them as the time and occasion demands. Surely a feeling of the unique will be generated if, when young, an actor can perform the style of an older man; or if an actor in later years can retain the presence he had in the prime of life. If he rises to a higher level of the art of Nō, but intentionally abandons and forgets his past styles, he will lose the seed of the Flower. Not retaining the seeds of the Flowers you obtained at various times in your life is like holding the flower of a branch you have broken off from the tree. But if you *do* keep the seeds, will the Flower not remain as the years and seasons progress? I must repeat: do not forget the mind you had in the beginning. Young actors are thus commonly praised as "rising quickly," or "seeming to be quite accomplished," while older men are praised as "appearing to be quite young." Is this not the principle of the unique? If you add some color to the various styles, their hues will multiply a hundred times. If, in addition, you can carry the various arts and abilities you have obtained over the years in your one single body, how astonishing will your Flower be?

In Nō, you should take care over a great number of things. Generally speaking, when giving a performance of someone who is angry, you must not forget to maintain a gentle mind. This is because no matter how far the anger goes, your method of acting should not become rough. Maintaining a gentle mind while expressing anger is the very principle of the unique. Again, in a role of graceful and subtle elegance, you should not forget the principle of strength. And so with everything—the dance, actions, role-playing—this is the principle of not being confined to the obvious. You should pay particular attention to the use of your body. When you are using your body with strength, you must stamp your feet in a hushed way. And when you stamp your feet with strength, you should carry your body peacefully. This is difficult to express in writing. It is an oral teaching from teacher to student. It can be seen in detail under the heading of Learning the Flower contained within the *Kakyō*.

The matter of knowing the "Hidden Flower" is contained in the statement, "If it is hidden, it is the Flower; if it is not hidden, it is not the Flower." Knowledge of this distinction is an essential of the Flower. First, in all things—Ways and arts—each clan has its own secret teachings because its greatest effects are dependent on that secrecy; yet, if these secrets are exposed, they do not appear to be worth being secretive about. However those who say that there is nothing much to these secrets do so because they have not yet understood the great efficiency of what we call secret teachings. First of all, in the oral traditions on the Flower it states that if everyone comes to understand that "the Flower is simply in the unique," then the audience will be expecting there to be something unique. Thus, even if there *is* something unique in the performance, it will not likely create an impression of being so in the expectant minds of those who are watching. An actor's Flower will appear because those watching are not expecting it. Thus, the audience may see something extraordinarily skillful and interesting, but will not know that it is the Flower, and this is precisely the actor's true Flower. In this way, the Flower is that method which draws out a feeling that people had not expected to have.

In the martial arts, for example, a great general will

defeat a strong enemy by means of some unexpected method in his strategy or judgment. In such cases, wasn't the losing side defeated because they were fooled by the principle of the unique? In all things—and all Ways and arts—this is the principle prevailing in victory or defeat. It is easy enough to understand such strategies and guard against them after the matter has been settled, but people are defeated because they didn't understand them beforehand. This is the nature of secret matters, and it is one thing we bequeath to our clan. You should understand these things accordingly: not only should you not reveal these secrets to others, but you should not even let others know that you yourself are someone who knows such secrets. If you let your opponent know what is in your mind, he will not be negligent—indeed, he will be on guard, and in the end you will cause him to be mindful of your intent. If you do not cause the enemy to be on guard, your victory will be all the easier. Causing others to be careless, and thus grasping the victory is the great use of the principle of the unique, is it not? To this extent, by not letting others understand that our clan has these secrets, you will be a master of the Flower for your entire life. If it is kept secret, there is the Flower; if it is not kept secret, there is no Flower.

Understanding the Law of Cause and Effect[55] in relation to the Flower is of the utmost significance. Everything—all things—contains the Law of Cause and Effect. All the many things you have learned about the art of Nō since you were a beginner are the cause. Mastering Nō and gaining a name for yourself is the effect. Thus if you neglect the cause of training, it will be difficult to bring the effect to fruition. You should understand this very well. Again, you should be exceedingly mindful of the passage of time. You should know that if you were in your prime last year, you will likely not have the Flower this year. At intervals there will be moments of good luck and moments of bad luck. No matter what you do, if there are good moments in Nō, there will also be bad. This is a matter of cause and effect, and there is nothing you can do about it. With this understanding, do not be too attached to your own aspirations during a competitive performance of Nō that is relatively unimportant. Give a moderate performance without exhaustive effort, do not be too worried about losing the contest, and do not use all of your techniques. The spectators may also wonder about what is taking place, and take only a light interest in your performance. For an important performance of *sarugaku*, however, change your methods, show your skilled capabilities, and act with diligence. If you do this, the spectators will be given an extraordinary impression; and in an important match or vital contest, your victory will be assured. This is the great function of the unique. In this way, what was bad karma becomes good.

Generally speaking, in *sarugaku* performances extending over three days at three different venues, manage yourself conservatively on the first day, and hold back on your techniques. For the day you consider to be the most important of the three, however, you should show your expertise and excellent capabilities, and leave the audience wide-eyed. Even in the case of a contest during a single day's performance, if you naturally encounter a moment of bad luck, hold back at first and, at the moment your opponent's good luck turns bad, put everything you have into your own capabilities. That moment will be the point when your luck turns good. If you perform well at the crux, you should take the first prize on that day. Moments of good and bad luck are predetermined, and color one side or the other in every contest. This gives each contest a critical time, which should be understood as the moment of good luck. If the contest is a long one with a number of plays, this moment of good luck will change from one side to the other. In a certain document it says, "When it comes to the gods of contest, there is a god of victory and a god of defeat. They are present at the contest, and provide for its outcome. This is a primary secret in the Way of the martial arts." If your opponent's *sarugaku* is performed well, you should understand that the god of victory is on his side, and be first and foremost respectfully mindful of this fact. Nevertheless, as there are two gods involved in these moments of the Law of Cause and Effect, they will change from one side to the other; and when you think that the moment is with you, you should perform with self-confidence. This is, then, the Law of Cause and Effect at the place of performance. I must repeat, do not take this lightly. "In your faith will be your virtue."[56]

So then, if you look exhaustively through this matter of good and bad moments in the Law of Cause and Effect, and leave no stone unturned, you will see that it is simply the two points of the unique and the not unique. The same Nō play may be performed by the same skilled actor both yesterday and today, and what was perceived as interesting yesterday will no longer hold any interest today. This is because yesterday's perception still remains in the spectator's mind. Thus today there seems nothing unique about the performance, and it merely seems poor. Later, however, when it is performed well once again, the same mind that thought it performed poorly before will now see it as something unique and interesting. When you delve exhaustively into this Way, you will see that this is precisely what the Flower is. If you do not delve into the deepest principles and understand that the principle of the unique is in everything, you will likely not have the Flower.[57] In the sutras[58] it says, "Good and bad are not two. The correct and the heretical are the same." Fundamentally, how can you determine what is good or what is bad? It is simply that, according to the moment, what is sufficient for use is considered something good, and what is insufficient is considered bad. The many different varieties of our style respond to the many people in our world and range over a multitude of places. Thus, a certain style is performed to the broad tastes of the time, and this is the Flower that is sufficient for use. Although one style may bring pleasure here, another will be praised in yet a different place. In this way, the Flower changes from person to person and from mind to mind. In which one is the absolute truth? You will only know the Flower by what can be used at the time.

This separate oral teaching concerning our art is extraordinarily important to our clan, and should be conferred to only one person every generation. It should not be given to someone without talent, even if he is your child. As the saying goes, "A birthright is not the clan. The clan is the handing down of the art. A man is not necessarily *the* man. It is knowledge that makes him so." Through these teachings you should attain that delicate Flower of the enlightenment of ten thousand virtues.

Some years ago I passed these separate articles on to my younger brother Shiro, but they may be given to Mototsugu[59] or others who are talented in the art of Nō. This is an extremely secret transmission.

Twenty-fifth year of Oe[60]
First day of the Six Month
Zeami

NOTES

1. The "land of the Buddha" refers to India, while the "Age of the Gods" refers to the Japanese creation myths.
2. The present-day cities of Nara and Ōtsu, respectively.
3. Note that a child's age was calculated as starting at age one from the time of birth.
4. Nishio Minoru defines the true Flower as "The Flower that has come into existence through exhaustive practice and effort; it is a Flower that does not fall." The Flower of the moment is one that "appears according to the actor's age, and falls after that age has passed." (Nogami & Nishio, *Fūshikaden*, 14)
5. Evening practice should use a strong full voice; morning practice should be more reserved. (Hayashi, *Surasura yomeru Fūshikaden*, 25)
6. Of the twelve basic pitches in ancient court music, *ōshiki* is number eight and *banshiki* number ten, respectively. (Nogami & Nishio, *Fūshikaden*, 15)
7. Zeami uses the Buddhist term *kahō* (果報), which can mean a reward or retribution for former actions.
8. The text here would seem to indicate that "not doing it" (*senu*, せぬ) would simply mean "not getting involved." But this particular term is very important in Zeami's theories on Nō, and should be mentioned here. In the *Kakyō* he states (Nose, *Zeami jūroku būshū hyōshaku*, vol. 1, 375–6):

    In the criticism of observers it is said that "the place where nothing is done (*senu tokoro*, せぬところ) is interesting." This is the *shite*'s greatest secret, concentration of mind. First there is chanting and dance, then the various roles all of which use techniques performed by the body. What I call "the place where nothing is done" refers to the intervals between these things. For these intervals where "nothing is done" to be interesting to the audience, there must be no unguarded moment, and the actor's mind must be drawn as tight as hoops around a barrel. In the interval after the dance is finished, or where the chanting has ceased, or in the intervals between all the various activities like speaking or role-playing, the concentrated mind must not be abandoned. Instead, one should be deeply circumspect. When this sensation deep within the mind is sensed from without [by the audience], it is extremely interesting. Yet, it is no good when this inner mind can be seen from the outside. If it can be seen, it is simply technique; it is not "doing nothing." When you have reached the level of "no-mind," your concentrated mind will be hidden even from yourself, thus binding everything that comes before or after to these intervals of "doing nothing." This refers precisely to the intuitive power that binds all skills together with the concentrated mind.

9. Ch'i-lin was a famous horse in ancient China that could run a thousand *ri* in one day.

10. 1384.

11. An ancient province which included the modern city of Shizuoka, where the Sengen Shrine is located.

12. Either a kimono or an article of clothing worn over the upper half of the body.

13. A sort of ceremonial pant-skirt.

14. A wadded silk kimono-style garment.

15. A dance done to the accompaniment of a narrative chant and a hand-held drum.

16. Ashura: these are the warring gods of one of the Six Worlds in the Buddhist universe into which we are reincarnated in our next life, depending on our actions in this one. A warrior would be born into the world of the Ashuras, or even considered to be in it already. Since the Ashuras are constantly fighting, their world is a dubious choice.

17. The Minamoto (Genji) and Taira (Heike) clans fought for supremacy during the twelfth century in Japan, the Minamoto emerging as the victors. A number of literary works covered this conflict, including the classic *Tale of the Heike* and a number of Nō plays.

18. The *jo* 序, *ha* 破, and *kyū* 急 indicate stages of development or movement. They could be translated as the introduction, the change, and the impact respectively. Originally terms used for traditional Japanese music, they have been adopted by many of the Japanese arts, included linked poetry, court football, Nō, and the martial arts. Makoto Ueda (*Literary and Art Theories in Japan*, 69–70) states "The structure of the Nō is musically conceived: it has *jo*, *ha*, and *kyū*, like traditional Japanese music. The rhythm of the Nō play is suggestive of the great hidden law of the universe; it is, in fact, the universal rhythm of life."

19. Both Chinese and Japanese poetry and prose were written at the time, and Zeami makes a clear distinction between them.

20. *Inu-zakura*: Either the cherry laurel (*Prunus spinulosa*) or the bird cherry (*Prunus grayana*); generally considered the least spectacular of the cherry blossoms. (Kuitert, *Japanese Flowering Cherries*, 28)

21. "If I am in the company of three people, they will invariably become my teachers. I take what is good from the good man and follow it; through the man who is not good, I reform myself." The Analects (Kanaya, *Rongo*, 7:21).

22. With Zeami, this term (*kurai*, 位) may also be understood as something like "loftiness," and the reader should keep this in mind while reading this section.

23. Poem 340 in the *Shin kokin wakashū*, the eighth imperial anthology, compiled in 1205. The poem was written by Fujiwara Kiyosuke (1104–77).

24. Poem 797 in the *Kokin wakashū*, the first imperial anthology, compiled in 905. The poem is by Ono no Komachi (c. 850), a poetess known for her astonishing beauty.

25. Hui-neng (638–713), the sixth patriarch of Ch'an (Zen) Buddhism

in China. The quote can be found in the Platform Sutra of the Sixth Patriarch.

26. The year 1400 by the Western calendar. Zeami was thirty-eight years old at the time.

27. An honorary title accompanying the name Saemon Dayū, conferred on Zeami to allow him to enter the royal palace.

28. This character (秦) is pronounced both "hada" and "hata." In Nogami & Nishio, it is given the former pronunciation. It seems to have been a name given anciently to naturalized foreigners. Motokiyo is Zeami's given name, while the name Hada identifies him as a direct descendant of Hada no Kōkatsu.

29. Ama no Uzume's dance may have been slightly risqué. It is said that as she danced, she pulled down the top of her blouse and pulled up her skirt, causing the gods to howl with laughter. It was this laughter that piqued Amaterasu's curiosity, and enticed her to push away the boulder in front of the cave.

30. This was the famous Jetavana monastery in Shravasti, India, where the Buddha spent nineteen rainy seasons.

31. Devadatta was a cousin and rival of the Buddha. He conspired to kill the latter at least three times, and eventually brought about a schism among the monks. He was condemned to suffering in the multiple hells of Buddhism, but according to certain sutras the Buddha himself prophesied his future enlightenment.

32. One of the Buddha's principle disciples, famous for his wisdom.

33. The cousin and personal attendant to the Buddha, Ananda was known for his humility, devotion, and memory. It was he who memorized all the Buddha's sermons, and set the beginning of each discourse with "Thus have I heard . . . "

34. One of the ten great disciples of the Buddha, famous for his eloquence in spreading the Dharma.

35. *Nyorai* (如来), meaning "Buddha," is the Sino-Japanese for the Sanskrit term *tathagata*, or "Thus Come."

36. Twenty-ninth emperor of Japan (509–71).

37. The emperor who united China under the Ch'in Dynasty. He was known for a strictness that easily bordered on cruelty (d. 210 B.C.).

38. Ōsake (大荒): in a village local to this area, there is an Ōsake Shrine said to be founded by the Hada family. In this case, however, *ōsake* is written with the characters 大酒, literally "big saké."

39. One of the guardian gods of the four directions, in this case, the north. In Sanskrit, Vaisravana.

40. Mononobe no Moriya (d. 587) was favored by the emperors Bitatsu and Yōmei, but opposed the introduction of Buddhism to Japan by the Soga clan. He burned down the first Buddhist temple and threw the images of the Buddha into the Naniwa Canal. Later, his entire family was destroyed by the Soga.

41. Modern-day Kyoto. The capital was moved there in 794.

42. *Kyōgen kigo* (狂言綺語): from a phrase by the Chinese poet Po Chu-i (772–846), in which he hopes that the excesses of his "crazy words and extravagant language" will have some "karmic connection with praising the Buddha in the future, and with turning the Wheel of the Law." Found in entry #588 in the *Wakan rōeishū* ("Japanese and Chinese Poems for Chanting") compiled around 1213 by Fujiwara Kintō, a book with which Zeami would have been familiar. See Kawaguchi, *Wakan rōeishū*, 440.

43. *Okina* means "old man."

44. According to Soothill, "the threefold body or nature of a Buddha, i.e., the Dharmakaya, Sambhogakaya, and Nirmanakaya . . . the Buddha-body *per se*, or in its essential nature; his body of bliss, which he 'receives' for his own 'use' or enjoyment; and his body of transformation, by which he can appear in any form." (*Dictionary of Chinese Buddhist Terms*, 77)

45. Every year at the Kōfukuji Temple, from October 10–17, there is a lecture and services based on the Yuima (*Vimalakirti* in Sanskrit) Sutra.

46. These are *takigi nō*, or performances of plays about gods, held on the lawn at night in the light of bonfires.
47. *Ishin denshin* (以心伝心): the Zen Buddhist phrase indicating that enlightenment is transmitted from mind to mind.
48. *Dengaku* originally developed as a folk art of dances with drum and flute music performed at rice planting, but became a respected art of its own. *Sarugaku* and *dengaku* seem to have been substantially influenced by each other.
49. See page 92.
50. 1402. Zeami was forty years old.
51. See page 85.
52. By "unreal fabrication," Zeami means role-playing that is not based on the true character of that role.
53. See page 97.
54. See chapter two, "Demons," page 80.
55. *Inga* (因果): Karma.
56. *Shin araba toku arubeshi* (信あらば徳あるべし): during Zeami's time, the character for "virtue" might also be understood as "strength," which gives the phrase a slightly different nuance.
57. Zeami was likely familiar with the Zen and tea ceremony saying that "each occasion (or meeting) is unique in one's life" (*ichigo ichie*, 一期一会).
58. Zeami appears to be referring to the above-mentioned Yuima Sutra, specifically the eighth chapter (the ninth chapter in some versions), which is concerned with non-dualism.
59. It is not absolutely certain who this is, but it may refer to Zeami's eldest son.
60. 1418. Zeami was then fifty-six years old.

GLOSSARY

Zeami wrote the *Fūshikaden* over a period of eighteen years. During that time it was perhaps inevitable that his feelings about certain concepts and the words used to express them would change—in nuance if not in basic meaning. Moreover, some of the most important aesthetic terms employed by Zeami had already been in use for centuries and had proven quite plastic according to the poet or critic applying them. Zeami inherited these accumulations of meanings and, as others before him, used them to express his own ideas. Just as today's performance did not have to conform to yesterday's, neither would certain concepts be constrained too tightly within definitional bonds. Thus Zeami's aesthetic vocabulary was fluid, and somewhat free. Like Miyamoto Musashi's handbook on swordsmanship, *The Book of Five Rings*, the purpose of the *Fūshikaden* was to insure the survival of the practitioner. This could not be done with rigid concepts and actions.

I have therefore included a limited glossary of the terms most important for an understanding of the *Fūshikaden*. Some may be quite clear, while others may offer a broad latitude of meanings. The reader is encouraged to refer to this glossary often as he or she reads through the book, and to keep in mind the range of meanings of each word as it is applied to the text.

Dengaku (田楽): lit. *den*, "rice field," + *gaku*, "music," "amusement," "joyful." This form of entertainment originated with music and dancing to celebrate the gods during rice planting, employing flutes and drums to attract the deities and thereby insure good crops. By the Heian period (794–1185), professional entertainers had started incorporating some aspects of *dengaku* into public amusements that included juggling, acrobatics, and mime. By Zeami's time, this "public" *dengaku* had reached the status of drama and was a rival to *sarugaku*.

Fūshi (風姿): "appearance" or "style," but Zeami uses it to mean something very close to "presence."

Fūtei (風体): a term often translated as "style," but which also means "atmosphere," "appearance," and "presence." In this last definition, it seems close to the term *fūshi*.

Hana (花): lit. "flower." One of Zeami's most central concepts in the *Fūshikaden*, which, however, he does not truly define. In the beginning of the text, *hana* seems almost to imply a kind of grace in a performance—physical, psychological, and spiritual—which impresses the audience with its unique quality. By the end of the treatise, it is more clearly a sensation evoked in the audience of the charm, interest, and uniqueness of the actor's performance.

Jo, **ha**, **kyū** (序, 破, 急): the artistic pattern of modulations of introduction, change, and impact, which, according to Zeami, is the rhythmic paradigm of the universe. In Nō, it is applied to the rhythm of both the chant and music, and to the sequential order of the plays. The concept is used by a number of arts in Japan, including swordsmanship.

Kagura: originally written 神座, or "seat of the gods," it is now written 神楽 to comply with its meaning of "entertainment of the gods." It is the sacred Shintō music and dance performed for worshipping the gods. According to the *Kojiki*, Japan's earliest written history, it was first danced by Ama no Uzume to entice the Sun Goddess Amaterasu from her hiding place in a cave. It is anciently connected with *sarugaku*.

Kakari: may be written with several different kanji, but Zeami used the *hiragana* syllabary (かかり). It refers to a way of expression, or a flavor or atmosphere that permeates that expression. In the music of Nō, it is often taken to mean the rhythm, but more probably indicates the atmosphere or mood of the rhythm. It can also indicate elegance or a certain aesthetic.

Kasa (かさ, also written as 嵩): breadth, dignity, or the beauty of sturdiness or vigor. In the *Fūshikaden*, Zeami defines it as a "form of stately authority." (See page 92.)

Monomane: written variously as 物学, "the study of things," and 物真似, "the truthful imitation of things"; although Zeami more often uses the kanji for *mono* (物) only, and leaves *mane* to the hiragana syllabary (物まね). *Monomane* is role-playing or mimicry, but is performed so as to represent not the simple actions of the character being portrayed, but their "true intent," their very deepest intrinsic nature. Zeami states that for true *monomane*, the actor must become the object of his role to the point where he is imitating by not imitating.

Nō (能): lit. "ability," "talent," or "capability," but by Zeami's time and in terms of his profession it also began to mean "performance." In the *Fūshikaden*, it sometimes means "ability," sometimes "performance," and sometimes "Nō." There are also cases when it would seem to incorporate all three meanings.

Sarugaku (申楽): the early form of Nō based on mime, chanting, music, and dance. When Zeami speaks of *sarugaku*, he is speaking fundamentally of Nō. *Sarugaku* has been defined at length in the introduction.

Shiore (萎れ): lit. "wilting" or "fading." The mood or pathos engendered when the flower begins to fade.

Shirabyōshi (白拍子): lit. "white rhythm." A song and dance popular between the Heian and Kamakura periods, performed by courtesans attired in the ceremonial white robes of the samurai, and accompanied by a drum and flute. The rhythms of this entertainment were found to be scandalous by some members of the aristocracy, but were incorporated artistically into *sarugaku* by Kan'ami.

Shite: the main actor or protagonist of the Nō drama. He is generally termed the *maejite* in the first half of the play, and the *atojite* or *nochijite* in the latter half. The *shite* performs the dancing and major chanting, especially in the second half of the play. He, and sometimes his *tsure*, often wear masks.

Take (丈 or 長): a word current since ancient times in Japanese aesthetics, meaning generally an imposing character. It would seem, however, to include a number of nuances, including "strength," "dignity," and "nobility." Zeami states that this quality is "inherent (*seitoku*, 生得), and different from *kasa*."

Tsure: those actors accompanying the *shite* and sometimes the *waki*. Their main function, other than as companions, is to take part in the chants.

Waka (和歌): lit. "Japanese poem." Also called *tanka*, this is the classic form of poetry in Japan, composed since very ancient times primarily by the court nobles, and still composed today. It is made up of thirty-one syllables in five lines of 5–7–5–7–7. Very simply put, its aesthetic is one of elegance and beauty, sometimes tinged with a mild melancholy.

Waki: the second most important actor of the Nō play, often described as the deuteragonist. He introduces the setting and the general direction of the play, and leads the *shite* in the dramatic chanting during the second part of the play.

Yūgen (幽玄): *yū* generally means "dim" or "hazily perceived"; *gen*, "something hidden in deep principles" or "mysteries not easily understood." In the Taoist philosophies of Lao Tzu and Chuang Tzu, *yūgen* indicates the profound, unfathomable, and subtle. In early Japanese poetic aesthetics, it meant the deep and unknowable, yet elegant in the pathos of things. Later, it began to mean a graceful and subtle beauty, and an elegant simplicity and gentleness with a touch of melancholy. Zeami inherited and was familiar with all of these meanings and nuances. It is important, however, to note that one of his most well-known statements about *yūgen*, found in his book *Kakyō*, relates that its "very essence lies simply in the beautiful and gentle." (Nose, *Zeami jūroku bushū hyōshaku*, vol. 1, 358) And in the *Shikadōsho* he notes, "A white swan with a flower in its bill; is this not the presence of *yūgen*?" (ibid., 478). For interesting discussions on *yūgen*, see Hisamatsu, *The Vocabulary of Literary Japanese Aesthetics*, 33–44; and Ueda, *Literary and Art Theories in Japan*, 55–71.

敦盛
ATSUMORI

Zeami

Mitsuhiro Honda of the Konparu school is the *shite* in a special performance of *Atsumori* at the National Noh Theatre, Tokyo, on 27 April 1995.

INTRODUCTION

The *Heike monogatari*, or "Tale of the Heike," was composed in its final form in the late thirteenth century, perhaps 1371, by Akashi Kakuichi. Too beautifully written to be called simply a war chronicle, it follows the Taira (Heike) clan from its rise in around 1156 to its quick and complete destruction at the hands of the Minamoto (Genji) clan in 1185. In this tale, many of the warriors are portrayed in terms of the classic ideal of the balance of *bun* (文) and *bu* (武), or the literary and the martial, and are often described as accomplished in poetry or some other art. A work of considerable length, the *Heike monogatari* was chanted for centuries by blind *biwa* players, who were often lay Buddhist priests. In the late fourteenth and fifteenth centuries, it was the source for a number of Zeami's most notable Nō plays.

The ninth book, sixteenth chapter of the *Heike monogatari* is the story of the death of Atsumori, an elegant young Taira warrior who was also a gifted musician. As the Taira were retreating, he returned to their deserted encampment to find the flute he had left behind. There he encountered an older and much stronger enemy warrior, Kumagai Naozane. Naozane captured Atsumori after a brief fight and was ready to cut off his head, when he was astounded to learn that his victim was just sixteen, his own son's age, and was the skilled flute player he had heard from his own camp the night before.

Inclined to spare the youth secretly, he suddenly heard his own allies approaching and knew that he had no choice but to kill him. After the war, Naozane became a Buddhist priest and returned to the spot of the tragedy to pray for Atsumori's soul. This story Zeami shaped into one of his most moving and beautifully written plays.

No doubt, the many warriors who studied Nō cherished and chanted this play over and over. The story contains much that would have been of interest to the warrior class spectator of this play: martial prowess matched with artistic talent, compassion, duty, and perhaps above all, concern for the soul after a life of battle and slaughter. It may be recalled that even before Zeami's time, secular literature was considered as strong an inspiration as the sutras for conversion to the Buddhist Way. Indeed, the very last line of this story in the *Heike monogatari* seems to invite the recitation of Zeami's work that was to follow it: "How moving that even the principles behind 'crazy words and extravagant language' may in the end be the cause of praise for the Buddha's teachings."*

---

* Takagi et. al., *Heike monogatari*, 222. The phrase "crazy words and extravant language" (*kyōgen kigo*, 狂言綺語) is the same as that of the T'ang dynasty poet, Po Chu-i, that Zeami quotes in the fourth chapter of the *Fūshikaden*. Although it is often noted that in the *Heike monogatari* these words refer to Atsumori's flute playing (and to secular literature in general) and how the music moved Naozane to become a priest, the meaning is the same from genre to genre, from Po to Akashi to Zeami, i.e. secular art can move men to religion.

ATSUMORI

[Enter the *waki*, the Buddhist priest Rensei.]

Waki: Aware now that the world is but a dream,
  aware now that the world is but a dream,
 forsake it and reality is manifest.

This man you see is the former resident of Musashi Province, Kumagai Jirō Naozane. Having renounced the world, I am now the Buddhist priest Rensei. Atsumori died by my hand, and I have taken on this guise in a surfeit of pain. Moreover, I am thinking now of traveling to Ichi-no-tani, to pray for Atsumori's salvation.

A moon emerging from the capital
  of many-layered clouds,
a moon emerging from the capital
  of many-layered clouds:
a tiny wheel
  revolving towards the south,

> beyond the Yodo waterway and Yamazaki,
> past Koya Pond and the Ikuta River.
> Waves pounding at Suma Bay,
> I have arrived at Ichi-no-tani
> arrived at Ichi-no-tani.

Having traveled so swiftly, I have arrived at Ichi-no-tani in the province of Tsu. Truly, the scene of long ago is brought back to me as though it were the present again. I hear the sound of a flute coming from the farther fields. I think I'll wait for its owner to appear and ask about the details of what happened here.

[The *shite*, Atsumori's spirit, now appears as a grass cutter. He is accompanied by three other grass cutters. All carry sprays of spring flowers as they enter the stage.]

Shite & tsure: Grass cutters accompanied by the songs of a flute,
  grass cutters accompanied by the songs of a flute;
  it is but the wild wind that blows.

Shite: The men who cut grass on this hill,[1]
  making their way through the fields,
  returning home at dusk.

Shite & tsure: The way home, indeed,
  the sea at Suma,
   a path of coming and going,
    not so long,
     for those entering the mountains,
     for those going out to the sea,
      work never-ending,
       the grief of things . . .

   If you should ask, I would answer,
   I grieve here alone[2]
     at Suma Bay,
    salt tears flowing,
      would that someone knew,
    salt tears flowing,
      would that someone knew,
   I, too, might have a friend.
   Yet, such is my ruin, even
     those intimate
      would shun me.[3]
   Thinking thus,
    to live like this,
   I give myself to grief
     and carry on,
   I give myself to grief
     and carry on.

[The *tsure* retire to the side, the *shite* moves to center stage, and the *waki* stands and faces him.]

Waki: Perhaps I should ask this grass cutter here.

Shite: Me? What do you want?

Waki: The flute I heard just now. Was it played by one of you?

Shite: Yes, it was played by one of us.

Waki: What a graceful sound: an artfulness beyond
        people of your station.
           A truly graceful sound.

Shite: I understand
   it is an artfulness beyond
     people of our station, but
it has been observed:
   "You should not envy those above you,
   nor despise those below."
And more,
   "The woodcutters' songs
     the herders' flutes,"[4]

Tsure: The grass cutters' flutes and the woodcutters' songs
 are sung by the poets;
 thus heard in the world
  are not so strange!

Waki: Truly, truly, this is sound.
 Ah, then,
  the woodcutters' songs,
  the herders' flutes,

Shite: the grass cutters' flutes,

Waki: the woodcutters' songs:

Shite: a melody to ease your way
  through this world of grief.

Waki: The chanting, too,

Shite: and the dance,

Waki: the flutes,

Shite: and the pleasure in all these.

Tsure: An artfulness due our station,

    soothing the heart,
        the bamboo floating
           to shore
    soothing the heart,
        the bamboo floating
           to shore.[5]

Little Branch,[6] Cicada-Fold,[7]
there have been many famous flutes like these.
The flute played by
    the grass cutter
    also has a name:
        the Flute of Green Leaves.

If this were the shore at Sumiyoshi,
you might think it to be a Korean flute.[8]
But as this is the salt burners' Suma
    think of it as
        the fishers' firewood remains,
    think of it as
        the fishers' firewood remains.

[The *tsure* withdraws.]

Waki: How strange!
           The other grass cutters have all gone home, but

Shite: you alone have stayed behind. Why is this?

Shite: Why, you ask?
           In the evening waves
       a voice of strength has come.
       Recite for me the Ten Invocations.[9]

Waki: To recite the Ten Invocations,
          an easy thing;
       but first tell me
          who you are.

Shite: In truth, I am someone
          linked to Atsumori.

Waki: "Linked?"
          Just hearing this
       brings back the past.
       Pressing my palms together in prayer,
          Namu Amida Bu.[10]

[The *waki* kneels on one knee and presses his palms together in prayer. The *shite* faces the *waki* and also presses his palms together.]

Waki & shite: If I should attain Buddhahood,[11]
　　　　　　 in all the worlds in the ten directions
　　　　　　 if sentient beings will call my name,
　　　　　　 I will accept them all, rejecting none.

Tsure:　　 Do not abandon me.
　　　　　　 Though a single recitation
　　　　　　　　 should suffice,
　　　　　　 how welcome it would be:
　　　　　　 praying for the dead,
　　　　　　　　 every morning,
　　　　　　　　 every night.
　　　　　　 Though I have not revealed my name,
　　　　　　 morning and evening you say your prayers.
　　　　　　 The name we spoke of is my own.
　　　　　　 With these parting words,
　　　　　　　　 his figure faded and was gone
　　　　　　　　 his figure faded and was gone.

Interlude (*Ai*)

[The *kyōgen* as a villager, and the *waki*, the priest Rensei.]

Kyōgen:　　The person you see here is one who lives on Suma Bay. Today I've come down to watch the passing boats, thinking it might cheer me up.

[He sees the priest.]

Well, here's a priest I haven't seen before. Where are you from?

Waki: I'm a priest from the capital. Are you someone familiar with this area?

Kyōgen: Yes, I'm rather a person of these parts.

Waki: If that's so, please first come closer; there's something I'd like to ask about.

Kyōgen: Yes, indeed. What sort of thing would you like to ask?

Waki: This might be something unexpected, but I've heard that this is the place where the Taira and Minamoto clans fought a battle, and that here the young Taira noble, Atsumori, met his end. Would you tell me what you know about this?

Kyōgen: Well, this *is* rather unexpected. Though I am someone who lives hereabouts, I know little of the details of such things. Nevertheless, since I have met you now for the first time, and you ask this of me, it would not be right for me to say that I know nothing at all. So I'll tell you generally what I know.

Waki: That would be most kind.

Kyōgen: So it happened that in the autumn of the second year of Juei,[12] the Taira were driven from the capital by Kiso Yoshinaka. They retreated here, but in order to destroy them the Minamoto split their own sixty thousand mounted warriors into two groups, and struck them down easily. The entire Taira clan scattered like falling leaves. Among them was Atsumori, a noble of the fifth rank, son of Tsunemori, the High Steward of Palace Repairs. He had come down to the shore to board the royal ship, but had forgotten his treasured flute, the Little Branch, back at the camp. He felt that it would be regrettable to leave this behind to be taken by the enemy. He went back to the camp, took the flute, and returned to the shore. All the warships, with the royal ship at their lead, had set sail, but his horse was strong, and he thought to make it swim out to the ships. Just as he urged his horse into the sea, a warrior from the province of Musashi, Kumagai

Jirō Naozane, opened his war fan and beckoned him back. In the end, Atsumori returned to the shore and grappled with the man as the waves beat on them. The men fell between their horses and, as Kumagai was a man of great strength, he quickly grasped Atsumori and held him down. He was going to take Atsumori's head, but when he removed the latter's helmet and looked, he saw that he was a youth of fifteen or sixteen with make-up and black-painted teeth—an astonishingly fine warrior, indeed. Naozane considered sparing the youth, but looked to his rear and saw that Doi and Kajiwara and ten mounted warriors were coming along behind. Kumagai said, "I would like to spare you, but as you can see, my allies are coming along with a large force. You will die by my hand, but I will earnestly pray for your soul." He cut off Atsumori's head, and inspected his body, only to find a flute wrapped in a brocade pouch at his waist. He showed this to his commanding officer, and all were impressed that this youth must truly have been sensitive, even among the nobility, to be carrying a bamboo flute at such a time. It is said that everyone shed tears on the sleeves of their armor. Later, Kumagai inquired after the youth's name and found out that it was Atsumori, an officer of the fifth rank, and son of Tsunemori.

Now I wonder if it is true what they say. It is told that Kumagai renounced the world and prays for the enlightenment of Atsumori's soul. But if he were that kind of man, he would have spared him at that time. Yet, he didn't spare him, so what they say cannot be true. If that Kumagai came around here, I'd kill him myself out of respect for Atsumori.

Well, this is the way I've heard it. But why is it that you were asking about this? I'm starting to feel a little uncertain.

Waki: You've been very kind to tell me this story. Now there is no reason for me to conceal myself. I am Kumagai Jirō Naozane. Having renounced the world, I have become the priest called Rensei, and have come here to pray for the enlightenment of Atsumori's soul.

Kyōgen: What! You're the Master Kumagai I've been talking about? I didn't know that at all. Please forgive me for the little story I just told you. Well, they say that that if there's good in the strong, there's also bad in the strong, but it could be the other way around, I suppose. I hope you'll go on praying for Atsumori's soul all the more.

Waki: Please don't be concerned; I'm not put out in the least. The reason I came here was to pray for Atsumori's soul, so I'll stay for a while and chant from our blessed sutra even more. I'll pray earnestly for his soul at the site of his remains.

Kyōgen: If that's the case, please lodge with me.

Waki: I'll be depending on you, then . . .

Kyōgen: With pleasure.

[The *kyōgen* departs.]

Waki: Because of this,
   I will pray for the dead.
Because of this,
   I will pray for the dead.
And recite the Buddhist litany
   all through the night.
For Atsumori I will recite
   the Buddha's Name,
     and pray still more

>   for his salvation
>   and pray still more
>   for his salvation.

[The *shite* returns, outfitted as the young warrior Atsumori at the time of his death.]

Shite: The plovers flying to and fro
>   over the shore at Awaji;
>   hearing their cries,
>   he awakens
>   the barrier guard at Suma.[13]
>   Who can it be?

[Turning to the *waki*.]

>   Rensei! What now?
>   It is Atsumori who comes!

Waki: How strange!
>   I have rung the bell,
>   recited the prayers,
>   without a moment for sleep.
>   Yet Atsumori has come.
>   Could this be a dream?

Shite: Why should this be a dream?
In order to cleanse the karma
of our world of appearances,
I appear before you now.

Waki: What kind of talk is this?
Chanting the Holy Name:
"One thought of Amida
destroys sins without number."[14]
I have recited the litany without pause,
exerted myself in prayers for the dead.
What kind of karma could there be, here
beside this windswept sea?

Shite: So deep, the sins brought to the surface.

Waki: An implication that I, too, may attain
the deliverance of Buddhahood.

Shite: This, too, great merit for the next life.

Waki: In former days, enemies.

Shite: Now once again, friends.

Waki: Friends . . .

Tsure: Ah, isn't this it?
          "Shake loose of evil friends,
              and call on virtuous enemies."
          This saying speaks of you.
              How I am blessed,
              how I am blessed.
          And now the words of your contrition,
              scattered as flowers.
          Let us talk all through the night,
          let us talk all through the night.

[The *shite* sits on a stool in center stage, facing the audience.]

          The flowers of spring
              rise to the tops of the trees,
          encouraging all to seek
              the highest enlightenment.
          The moon of autumn
              sinks to the bottom of the stream,
          Demonstrating transformation
              of sentient beings below.

Shite: Yet the gates of the entire clan
          stood side by side, our kinsmen,
          leaf-filled branches on the trees.

Tsure: Truly, it is the same:
 the white hibiscus flourishes
 for a single day.[15]
 And the Teaching
 encouraging the Good
 is rarely encountered.
 Life is only the moment
 of the spark's light
 from the flint.
 But those who think
 not on this, their lives,
 the very stuff of transience.

Shite: Those above will suffer
 when they fall.

Tsure: Prosperous and proud,
 what did they know?

[The *shite* leaves the stool, and dances.]

 Yet the Taira ruled the world
 little more than twenty years;
 truly a single generation,
 their passing
 but within a dream.

Then, in the Juei era[16]
(which should have meant long life and happiness)
the leaves of autumn scattered,
beckoned to the four directions
    by the wind and rain.
A single leaf, a ship reclining on the wafting waves,
to return not even in a dream.

    The caged bird yearning for the clouds,
    returning geese disarrayed in flight.

Skies unsettled
    as the traveler's robes.
Days pass,
    months and years,
        til in the returning spring
they encamped a while at Ichi-no-tani,
here, at Suma Bay.

Shite: But from the mountains behind,
    winds blew down,

Tsure: freezing the fields.
    And at the shore,
no ships arriving
    day or night.
Only the crying calls of plovers

    as tears wet our sleeves,
sleeping
    on the wave-drenched beach,
together with the fishermen
    in their huts.
Thus we waited, now like the people of Suma,
supported by pebbles,
shaded by pines.
As evening smoke arose, we spread
something called brushwood[17]
thinking of how we now lived
    in this place,
a mountain village called Suma:
    the entire clan
        becoming Suma folk.
            How sad!

[The *shite* pauses in the dance, and faces the *waki*.]

Shite: Well then, in the evening
          of the sixth day of the Second Month, my father,
          Tsunemori, gathered us together
          to sing *imayō*[18] and to dance.

Waki: Ah, it was the diversion
            of that evening,

> the enchanting sounds
> > of the flute
> > > from within the battlements.
> > We, the assailant force,
> > heard it in our camp.

Shite: That, indeed,
> was Atsumori,
carrying to the very end
> his bamboo flute.

Waki: It sounds a measured melody,

Shite: the songs and chants

Waki: in every voice

Tsure: raising their voices with the tune.

[The Dance.]

[The *shite* continues dancing and chanting.]

Shite: This done,
> first the royal ship,

Tsure: then the boats
of all the clan
    set to float.
Thinking not to miss the boarding,
I approached the shore.
But the royal ship
and the warrior ships
    had put far out to sea.

Shite: There was nothing to be done,
    there in the waves,
reining back my horse.
I had come to this appalling pass:
    this my state,
        now attacked.

Tsure: From behind
    Kumagai Jirō Naozane,
    "Don't run!"
Pursued, Atsumori
    turns his horse,
unsheathes his sword
    in pounding waves.

[The *shite* throws away his fan and draws his sword.]

> You could see them strike
> > twice, three times.
> But grappling
> > while still mounted
> > > they fall
> > > > on the shore, wave-beaten.

[The *shite* kneels.]

> > In the end, he struck,
> > > my life was lost;

[The *shite* stands.]

> > but the wheel of Karma
> > > has turned:
> > > > this is my enemy!
> > > And now I strike,
> > but the enemy, in deep kindness,

[The *shite* sits, facing the *waki*.]

> > has called the Buddha's Name
> > > in holy rite,
> > praying for the dead.

[The *shite* stands.]

> In the end, reborn,
>> together
> on the same lotus flower.
> The priest, Rensei,[19] lotus-born,
>> no longer is
>> the enemy.

[The *shite* tosses away the sword, and faces the priest with palms pressed together.]

Shite: Pray for me again,
                and yet again.
            Oh, pray for me again.

[At the last phrase, the *shite* stamps the final beat.]

NOTES

1. A reference to a poem by Kakinomoto no Hitomaro, #440 in the *Wakan rōeishū*.

   > You grass cutters
   >   on this hill,
   > do not cut so clean and clear.
   >   My lord will be coming through
   >   to feed it to his mount.

2. A reference to a poem by Ariwara no Yukihira, #962 in the *Kokin wakashū*.

   > If by chance
   >   someone should ask after me,
   > please answer that I grieve
   >   salt dripping from racks of seaweed
   >   here at Suma Bay.

3. From the introduction to the *Kokin wakashū*.

   > Yesterday some were prosperous and proud, but today they grieve in their lost world, and are shunned by those who used to be intimate with them.

4. A reference to a poem by Ki no Seimei, #559 in the *Wakan rōeishū*.

   > As the sun fades on the mountain road,
   > my ears are filled with the sounds of woodcutters' songs
   >   and herders' flutes.
   > As birds return to their homes near valley streams,
   > my eyes are waylaid by the misty hues of bamboo
   >   and pine.

5. The sound of flutes made from such bamboo is said to be especially beautiful.

6. The flute Atsumori was carrying when he was killed by Naozane. It was presented to Taira Tadanori by the cloistered Emperor Toba and handed down to Atsumori.

7. A flute presented to the court of the cloistered Emperor Toba from the Chinese. The bamboo joints, where twigs began to appear, had the appearance of cicadas.

8. Korean ships were once anchored at the Bay of Sumiyoshi.

9. The invocation *Namu Amida Butsu* is recited for the dying by a priest ten times before a person's death.

10. An abbreviation for *Namu Amida Butsu*, or "Praise to the Buddha Amitabha." Amitabha is the Buddha of the Western Paradise, where the believers of some Buddhist sects believe they will go after death.

11. Amitabha Buddha made a series of vows before reaching enlightenment, the most remembered of which is his vow not to enter Nirvana until all sentient beings did so.

12. 1184.

13. A reference to a poem by Minamoto no Kanemasa, #78 in the *Hyakunin isshu*.

> At the cries of the plover
>   passing to and fro
> over the island of Awaji,
>   how many nights has he awakened,
>   the barrier guard at Suma?

14. From the Ōjō Hon'en Sutra.

> One thought of Amitabha
> and countless sins are destroyed.

15. A reference to a poem by Po Chu-i, #291 in the *Wakan rōeishū*.

    > The pine lives for one thousand years,
    >   but in the end rots away.
    > The Rose of Sharon, for just one day,
    >   flourishes of its own.

16. 1182–84. The kanji used to name this era are 壽永, longevity and a long period of time, respectively.

17. The aristocratic Taira, used to their lives in the capital, would have been unfamiliar with anything so basic. This is an allusion to a similar quote in the *Tale of Genji*.

18. *Imayō* (今様): lit. "in the current style." These were popular folk songs current during the latter part of the Heian Period.

19. Rensei (also sometimes pronounced Renshō): written with the kanji 蓮生, meaning literally "Lotus-Born."

BIBLIOGRAPHY

Works in Japanese

Amano Fumio. *Nō ni tsukareta kenryokusha.* Tokyo: Kodansha, 1997.

Baba Akiko. *Koten wo yomu: Fūshikadensho.* Tokyo: Iwanami Shoten, 2003.

Goto Hajime. *Nō no keisei to Zeami.* Tokyo: Mokujisha, 1966.

Hasegawa Tadashi, ed. and trans. into modern Japanese. *Taiheiki, shinpen Nihon koten bungaku zenshū,* vol. 54. Tokyo: Shōgakukan, 1994.

Hayashi Nozomu. *Surasura yomeru Fūshikaden.* Tokyo: Kodansha, 2003.

Kanaya Osamu, ed. *Rongo.* Tokyo: Iwanami Shoten, 1962.

Kanze Sakon. *Kanze-ryū yōkyoku hyakubanshū.* Tokyo: Hinoki shoten, 1973.

Kato Shuichi & Omote Akira, eds. *Zeami, zenchiku: Nihon shisō taikei,* vol. 24. Tokyo: Iwanami Shoten, 1998.

Kawaguchi Hisao, ed. *Wakan rōeishū.* Tokyo: Kodansha Gakujutsu Bunko, 1982.

Kawase Kazuma, ed. & trans. into modern Japanese. *Kadensho.* Tokyo: Kodansha, 1972.

Kojima Noriyuki & Arai Eizo, eds., *Kokin wakashū.* Tokyo, Iwanami Shoten, 1974.

Mizuno Satoshi, ed. and trans. into modern Japanese. *Fūshikaden.* Tokyo: PHP, 2005.

Mizuno Yahoko, ed. *Shōbōgenzō,* vol. 1. Tokyo: Iwanami Shoten, 1990.

Nagata Bunshōdō Henshūbu, ed. *Kongō-kyō.* Tokyo: Nagata Bunshōdō, 1956.

Nishino Haruo & Takenishi Hiroko. *Nō, kyōgen, Fūshikaden.* Tokyo: Shinchosha, 1992.

Nishio Minoru. *Zeami no nōgeiron.* Tokyo: Iwanami Shoten, 1974.

Nogami Toyoichiro & Nishio Minoru, eds. *Fūshikaden*. Tokyo: Iwanami Shoten, 1991.

Noma Seiroku. *Kosode to nō ishō, Nihon no bijutsu*, vol. 16. Tokyo: Heibonsha, 1965.

Nose Asaji, ed. *Zeami jūroku bushū hyōshaku*, vols. 1 & 2. Tokyo: Iwanami Shoten, 1940.

Shinkai Nagafusa, ed. *Zeami to nō no kokoro*. Tokyo: Kaishoten, 1941.

Shirasu Masako. *Zeami*. Tokyo: Kodansha, 1999.

Takagi Ichinosuke, Ozawa Masao, Atsumi Kaoru & Kindaichi Haruhiko, eds. *Heike monogatari*, vol. 2. Tokyo: Nihon Koten Bungaku Taikei, 1960.

Yokomichi Mario & Omote Akira, eds. *Yōkyoku shū*, vol. 1. Tokyo: Iwanami Shoten, 1943.

Works in English

Blyth, R. H. *Haiku, vol. 1: Eastern Culture*. Tokyo: Hokuseido Press, 1949.

de Poorter, Erika. *Zeami's Talks on Sarugaku*. Leiden: Hotei Publishing, 2002.

Gill, Robin D. *Topsy-Turvey, 1585*. Key Biscayne: Paraverse Press, 2004.

Gill, Robin D. *Rise, ye Sea Slugs!* Key Biscayne: Paraverse Press, 2003.

Hall, J.W. & Toyoda Takeshi, eds. *Japan in the Muromachi Age*. Berkeley: University of California Press, 1977.

Hisamatsu Senichi. *The Vocabulary of Japanese Literary Aesthetics*. Tokyo: Centre for East Asian Cultural Studies, 1963.

Kato Shuichi. *A History of Japanese Literature*, vols. 1 & 2. Tokyo: Kodansha International, 1983.

Kuitert, Wybe. *Japanese Flowering Cherries*. Portland: Timber Press, 1999.

La Fleur, William R. *The Karma of Words*. Berkeley: University of California Press, 1983.

O'Neill, P.G. *Collected Writings of P.G. O'Neill*. Tokyo: Japan Library & Edition Synapse, 2001.

Ortolani, B. & Leiter, S.L. *Zeami and the Nō Theatre in the World*. New York: CASTA, 1998.

Philippi, Donald. *Norito*. Princeton: Princeton University Press, 1990.

Red Pine. *The Heart Sutra*. Washington, D.C.: Shoemaker & Hoard, 2004.

Rimer, J.T. & Yamazaki Masakazu. *On the Art of Nō Drama*. Princeton: Princeton University Press, 1984.

Souyri, Pierre Francois. *The World Turned Upside Down*. New York: Columbia University Press, 2001.

Suzuki, D.T. *Zen and Japanese Culture*. New York: Bollingen Foundation, 1959.

Tyler, Royall. *Japanese Nō Dramas*. London: Penguin Books, 1992.

Ueda Makoto. *Literary and Art Theories in Japan*. Ann Arbor: University of Michigan, 1991.

Yagyū Munenori. *The Life-Giving Sword*. Trans. by William Scott Wilson. Tokyo: Kodansha International, 2003.

Works in English and Chinese

Blyth, R.H. *Zen and Zen Classics, vol. 4: Mumonkan*. Tokyo: Hokuseido Press, 1966.

Soothill, William Edward. *A Dictionary of Chinese Buddhist Terms*. Taipei: Ch'eng Wen Publishing Company. 1970.

(英文版)風姿花伝　The Flowering Spirit

2006年3月27日　第1刷発行

著　者　　世阿弥
訳　者　　ウィリアム・スコット・ウィルソン
発行者　　富田　充
発行所　　講談社インターナショナル株式会社
　　　　　〒112-8652 東京都文京区音羽1-17-14
　　　　　電話　03-3944-6493（編集部）
　　　　　　　　03-3944-6492（マーケティング部・業務部）
　　　　　ホームページ　www.kodansha-intl.com

印刷・製本所　　大日本印刷株式会社

落丁本・乱丁本は購入書店名を明記のうえ、講談社インターナショナル業務部宛にお送りください。送料小社負担にてお取替えします。なお、この本についてのお問い合わせは、編集部宛にお願いいたします。本書の無断複写（コピー）、転載は著作権法の例外を除き、禁じられています。

定価はカバーに表示してあります。

Printed in Japan
ISBN 4-7700-2499-1